A Child Inside

*understanding, healing and
freedom following childhood
abuse and trauma*

Sharon Shaw

Clink
Street

London | New York

Published by Clink Street Publishing 2018

Copyright © 2018

First edition.

ISBN:s 978-1-912262-72-4 paperback, 978-1-912262-73-1 ebook

Dedications

To a woman who loves, who showed me to love in many ways, who has even sacrificed herself in many ways to love. I have learnt so much and will continue to learn from you... I wouldn't be here and who I am now if you hadn't of loved me, guided me and listened to me. I have been blessed, love you Mother.

To my tutors and counsellor who taught me a language and guided me in seeking completeness, through self understanding and self love...in loving and accepting me in all that I was and now am.

I love my life, my past and my present, I appreciate all of my interactions with everyone, family, friends, acquaintances, strangers of all ages and race I have had the pleasure to meet so far in my life including the men that have done any wrong doing to me. I have learnt so much from everyone and I will continue to learn. I am truly sorry to anyone I have hurt in anyway verbally with my words or actions. I know my future is going to be amazing because I am going to move with peace, love and happiness, I will not succumb to pain, hate or fear, as I will always seek to understand it all and heal. For me this is Working Towards Complete Freedom a process that will never end because I will always be experiencing in every way, especially now that I am truly present in fully living my life in more self-awareness.

I find this really hard to say because I feel it was a man that broke me in parts but yet I found myself in a man. A man that was honest, not in what I wanted him to be honest about as it was sexual that linked into the man that first broke me. However within time and with reflection I acknowledged that his honesty gave me something that I was missing in my past experiences within men. This man's honesty showed me other deeper qualities that a man could hold or that could develop to hold, such as honesty, respect, independence, communication, equality and fairness towards a woman. I acknowledge now that my experience with him helped me to move to seek these qualities within other men. My hero did come just not in the fairytale way, the way I had learnt he would. I also acknowledge now that my need of a man to show me love meant that my future would be with the wrong man. I now know I am the woman I am because of these connections with this man. I will always be eternally grateful for my experience and what I have learnt from this man. Thank you Rick you were my hero, my knight in shining armor or should I say my shining eyes.

x

Introduction

Who am I? That is the question my counsellor was asking me. I started to reel off I am a Mum, a partner, a friend, a daughter, and I started to feel frustrated at the time it was taking me to show myself, frustrated with my chosen language, frustrated with my mind taking full control. I needed to 'be', not to be defined. The more I tried to define myself the more frustrated I became. Until I searched within, meaning I listened to my heart and intuition and found words that would give me movement, growth, and completeness. I said, "I am an essence that is everything; I am my past, my present and my future. My past is my present and my present is my future, 'myself'.

On reflection I perceive and feel that I am living two lives, a spiritual and a physical life. I perceive this last sentence to be contradictory to what I have just said, but it feels important to define and split myself; but not for me or you to get lost in the definitions as I know they all are very much me, in the hope that it will help you to understand my story, as this is what I did and continue to do to gain personal insight. To define it even further I perceive and feel my spiritual 'self' to be my true feelings, a knowing, insight interlinked with feeling and thought and my physical 'self' to be a thought first and then constructed feeling or feelings which are interlinked and are created from my thought. I believe these constructed thoughts were 'conformed' through significant others i.e. parents, family, teachers, friends, friends' parents, who I believe have also been 'conformed' from decades of cultural and societal ideology, just like Rogers (1951) believed. I perceive that these definitions are all interlinked

1

and are in effect just one; they interlink to make me who I am. Furthermore I now acknowledge that these thoughts and ideologies couldn't be conformed without me making a choice and I now know that as a child who was frightened of not being loved, so I chose to follow others (adults, parents, teachers, friends etc) but I made this decision through lack of self-awareness. I didn't have enough experience of life, self-understanding of my thoughts or feelings to make a decision that would benefit me as a whole being, to keep developing with balance.

I detect which one is my spiritual 'self' and which one is my physical 'self' through the movement of the whole of my body, for instance my intuition or 'spiritual self' I acknowledge is directed through my gut, a feeling of something churning in my stomach, a sense that the only way I can describe it as I am here but not here, a knowing that something more has happened, is happening, or will happen and a physical reaction where I either freeze, flight or fight. I acknowledge that when I detect these signals I move to be fully internal, seeking within, in my 'spiritual self', I suppose you could say in a trance-like state (hypnotised). This communication comes through my heart to my 'physical self', my brain in many different ways, now I acknowledge this has depended upon my cognitive development. You see as a child I acknowledged that it was more in a sensory way, but there was still communication, not necessarily verbal or formulated cognitive communication but a knowing that instructed me something was going to happen but that I would be OK. My physical reaction at that time was to freeze. I was there but not there (connected to sexual abuse when I was 6 years old). Whereas I remember another time when I was about 4 or 5 years old and some youths came into the shop and destroyed the shop; I quickly verbalised to my Mum that 'they were naughty' (a fight response). However my Mum was in a freeze response, telling me to be quiet. I didn't understand why and I believe on reflection because I had no fear, my cognitive brain had not developed enough to create fear. Whereas at 6 years old I acknowledge now I had fear that interlinked with adults, their disapproval and whether I would be loved or not, whether I would be punished or praised.

I acknowledge that I have grown and developed cognitively, emotionally and experimentally, reflecting moving internally to understand all of myself. The more I listen to my 'spiritual self' the clearer the communication is. I acknowledge that my 'spiritual self' moves in different ways and, I believe, interlinks universally to communicate with me. Therefore I have and do experience that not only do I experience internal feelings and thoughts connected to my 'spiritual self', I also experience things or see physical things to give clarity or reassurance of what my spiritual self is telling me.

To interlink this into life experience, I was with an ex-partner for 14 years with whom I have two beautiful daughters too and lots of cherished memories with. However on reflection I kept on having feelings that kept communicating to me that he and I were at different levels of life experiences, 'spiritual experiences', and 'physical development' indicating to me that the relationship would not last. However I kept denying that part of myself; on reflection I believe I denied that part of myself because I had chosen as a child not to trust that part of 'myself' and I had moved to believe more in my thoughts that are created from only my brain, from life experiences, and moved to put my trust in significant others first that they knew what was best for me. Sometimes I would stay with myself, but my decisions would be heavily influenced by people I trusted. I know this split in 'myself' developed from my early childhood experiences of sexual abuse, parent separation and loss of significant attachments where I blamed my 'spiritual self' from not saving me from those experiences. Just before I was sexually abused an internal voice told me something was going to happen that wouldn't be very nice, but that I would be OK. So within my relationship with my ex-partner I chose to ignore this deep feeling and communication, putting it down to insecurities connected to my past experiences of men.

As a metaphor you could perceive me to be like a double oven/grill, I need to understand how the oven/grill works in order to prepare and deliver the best food or in order for me 'to be the best that I can be' (Rogers, 1951). However for many years I didn't understand the spiritual me (the feeling, knowing) and unknowingly I repressed that part of myself and I believe that through me doing this I eventually became stuck, I stopped growing, I had grown as far as I could living just as the physical me (cognitive me). I had stopped living as a complete whole (thought, feeling and intuition) or as Rogers (1951) put it 'a fully functioning person'. I lived and developed more cognitively, repressing my true feelings and intuition.

My perceptions and beliefs were more constructed by my parents and significant adults, whom I perceive now to have been also conformed culturally and socially, due to what I perceive to be an imbalance of power (Proctor 2002). So in other words, the oven/grill was and could be used by others to prepare and deliver food, but they only knew how to use the grill (construction of thoughts and behaviour) not the oven (the spiritual experience of life/wisdom). As a child I allowed others (I didn't realise at this time) to keep on only using my grill (directing me in what to think and how to behave) which eventually broke. I had developed to only show and live as half of me, so that I eventually became depressed or as Rogers, (1951) would say I moved away from my 'true self', and this gap is what he called 'incongruity'. To give further understanding of this process I need to share my story but before I start, I want to explore why I am writing this book.

I understand that my personal process is a cycle in order for me to feel complete. I seek to be more understanding of my feelings, thoughts and behaviour therefore I am writing this book to help complete me. Well, it is cheaper than bringing all of this to a counsellor! I am also trying to show the essence of me through my story, definitions and metaphors in hope that by me sharing my story, 'my-self' will in the end entwine us so that you might start to see you in any of the experiences, thoughts and emotions I share. I hope to inspire you to follow your own process, to start to believe in yourself and seek whatever it is you want to know. I have experienced and am experiencing an awakening and I would love for you to experience it too. I desire to change for the better and I want to guide and help other people on their individual journey.

What I am not saying is that what I did and my process of analysis is the way to truth for everyone. What I desire is to share honestly all that I have experienced, all that I have observed, and my analysis of all that interlinked with all that I was and all that I am. I acknowledge that this desire of wanting to share was formulated from an internal conversation or analysis when I was a young child. I was sat in my bedroom thinking about the world and my experiences of life so far; I was wondering to myself why people would hide their feelings, why people would not tell the truth about what they were thinking and feeling. My intuition was telling me life would be so much easier, people would be happier as people would love themselves and others. I acknowledge that at that time I felt frustrated with not understanding what I was witnessing and observing from my life. For me at that time it seemed so simple, to be honest, open and share with others all that you are. That is when I made a promise to myself, that I would always tell my truth, that when I would become an adult I wouldn't lie to children, I wouldn't lie to anyone. I would share all of my thoughts and feelings, I wasn't going to become lost in lies, I wasn't going to shut children up, I wasn't going to make them feel less powerful, I would remember what it was like to be a child, remember how hard it was to express myself verbally finding words, to be heard, to be seen and to be understood. Little did I know what life would have in store for me. I was about to find out why people lie, hide and don't share all of themselves.

These personal promises all changed when I developed more cognitively and experienced traumatic experiences in childhood.

Chapter 1

Unconditional Love

My first ever memory as a child was in my mother's arms while she was feeding me a bottle and stroking my face. The feelings I were experiencing were contentment, love and peace. Then there are many short memories where I would be playing on my own or with my siblings and friends, and the strongest feeling I have when I go back to these early memories is of love and freedom. I have re-remembered this feeling all the way through my life, meaning from specific points in my life I have forgotten those feelings, then I have life experiences where I experience those feelings and this helps me re-remember that I used to experience them a lot as a young child.

From the age of six, I was sexually abused by a neighbour. When I go back to recall the first ever time the abuse started, all I can recall is images – there are no thoughts, but a strong feeling or knowing that told me something was going to happen but that I would be OK. I was frozen, like I was there but not there, and my perpetrator directed me in what to do. I wasn't frozen with fear though, it was a feeling or knowing it wasn't right but not that I was frightened.

I struggled for a long time as an adult to accept this feeling, as every time I went back as my adult self, I could not comprehend anything other than a six-year-old child to be frightened of a man getting them to perform sexual acts on him.

I remember that I didn't like it, but I liked him tickling my back and he had said that he had done something nice for me so now it was my turn to do something nice for him.

On reflection I had never experienced anything like that before, so I had nothing to compare it to and my perpetrator was my friend's Dad who used to buy me sweets and be nothing but kind. So why would I be frightened? He never acted nasty or angry!

After the sexual act he had told me that if I told anyone, my parents would die and I would never see my parents again.

This is when I first became frightened and I consider that it was because I had a cognitive understanding, not only from him, that death meant that I would never see my parents again. But I still perceive that at that moment I was not frightened of him.

I carried on going round to my friend's house and took sweets off him and let him tickle my back for about a year, even though I didn't like what he asked of me.

I perceive that at this point in time I hadn't developed cognitively enough to understand the connection of sweets, my back being tickled and his reward, or how to predict and forward think. It was like I kept forgetting, then I would get that strange feeling again. I was like a dog where you could have done anything and I would have still liked you. I consider that at this time I was not cognitively aware so I was easily manipulated; what was instilled inside of me was that adults were always right and that I should respect my elders, they were more powerful because they were older and knew better. This type of individual, cultural and societal belief is still instilled in children every day and it is ingrained within our systems and education system.

I remember being more cognitively aware one day when my perpetrator had brought us (me and his daughter) an ice cream and asked me to go and watch TV. I felt a knowing again of danger and I remember then feeling fear that I really didn't want to go into his house.

When I reflect back to analyse this experience I perceive that at this time I felt frightened as I could remember what was to come – or could potentially come, as it didn't happen all the time.

I consider that this feeling was created through my thoughts, as I was able to remember and my cognitive development was allowing me to be able to forward think to what might happen if I went into his house or if I said no to going into his house. I believe I formulated these thoughts on my experience of having an intuitive emotion before and my past experience of him abusing me. However, on reflection I also acknowledge that I formulated other thoughts from my observations of the world around me, other adults, and other experiences.

A thought that I had formulated told me that I could potentially experience what I had experienced before (sexual abuse) and I consider this thought to have been formulated from my knowing and my past experience of the abuse. Another thought that I formulated was that I could possibly get told off (by him or other adults) for being ungrateful or disobeying an adult. On reflection, I consider that I had formulated this thought from outside of me, other people/ cultural and societal rules and my experience of observing other people's interactions if rules were broken. Both thoughts presented fear as I didn't want to get told off nor did I want to experience what I had experienced.

I felt powerless that I had no choice but to do what he had asked.

On reflection, I perceive that my cognitive development was limited as I was a child and couldn't at this time think of another way around the situation as I didn't have enough life experience.

As I reflect back, I perceive that this was one of the first times I experienced an internal conflict where my thought and feeling overrode my intuition, my 'spiritual self'. I knew what was happening to me was wrong, my intuition or my heart was telling me it was wrong

or that there was danger. However, the thoughts that I had con-
formed from my experience of external sources were telling me that
there was also danger if I disobeyed an adult. My fear of being told
off or disobeying an adult and the punishment I could receive was
stronger than me not listening to myself, than me not loving myself.
This was the first of many times I chose to walk away from myself,
from listening to myself, my feelings, my spiritual self in order to
meet with the outside world, meaning other people's thoughts, feel-
ings, cultural and societal rules and regulations but without know-
ing the personal consequences of my actions.

On reflection, I acknowledge that my decision to walk away from myself or as Rogers (1951) puts it 'true-self' was reinforced by a situation where I experienced escaping from my perpetrator.

This day I recall really wanting to play with my friend but I was hesitant, because I felt that knowing and I was more aware of what I could potentially experience.

I can't fully remember my thought process at that time, I just
remember calling for her and experiencing the knowing feeling
getting stronger, and her Dad answering the door.

I asked if my friend was in, he said no, she had gone to the shop but I could come in and wait; with that, I replied I couldn't because my Mum didn't know where I was and she would be worried. He just said OK.

I remember walking away thinking I was ace, that my brain was
brilliant and feeling excited and relieved that I had managed to
escape. I do recall my analysis and thinking my thoughts were more
powerful than this stupid feeling that didn't really do a lot; it didn't
protect me.

As I walked home I met with my friend when she was coming back from the shop and we played and had a great time.

At this time my family life was full of love and I felt safe and secure with my three siblings, Mum and Dad. There was rivalry between us children, the general stuff, jealousy, the unfairness of someone getting that little bit more but all of us really got along really well with each other and I always remembered feeling privileged that I had siblings. That was probably because of my Mum always instilling it in us, that we always have each other to play with if friends are not playing. Also I remember that if I fell out with one of my siblings then I had two more to choose from so it was OK, but I also recall that I enjoyed time on my own, play-acting out my experiences of life, and other people's, being a Mum, having a boyfriend/husband etc. and wondering about life, why we were here and where did we come from.

So much so that at about seven years of age I remember feeling very fearful of death. This could obviously be to do with my experience of sexual abuse and the threat that if I ever told then my parents would die, but I do feel it sits deeper than that. I remember trying to understand what would happen if I died, and where would I go? Thinking to myself, if I die then everyone will die, believing that the world couldn't carry on without me. I recall also experiencing a recurring dream that I would die and people were there in capes saying I needed to go back as I had not learnt what I needed to learn, that I was me but an older me and I could fly and ants were my friends. I suppose what I am saying is that I have always remembered from childhood living another life, an internal life where I tried to understand my experiences of this physical world. These memories have always stayed with me but as I grew I repressed them, I chose not to remember and chose not to believe in them, believe in me... why?

The abuse carried on a few more times, but I got cleverer and found ways to escape and then I found a new friend. A friend who was not afraid of anything or anyone. Her name was Melanie. We became best friends, never leaving each other's side, laughing all the time.

I think that I had always been told that Melanie was poorly but I didn't really comprehend how poorly.

As I am saying this, my intuition is telling me that I always knew she wouldn't be here for long but cognitively I didn't understand.

I can remember being eight years old and her Mum picking me up from walking home from the shop, saying that Melanie was in hospital and my Mum said I could go and visit her. When I saw her I had a knowing, but cognitively I couldn't make sense of it; I remember her Mum saying try to be cheerful to make Melanie happy. I can remember being confused because I didn't see that Melanie was sad, I wasn't sad. I was excited to play with my friend, we played and laughed until it was time to say goodbye, it was a goodbye like any other goodbye, I will see you soon.

From what I can recall, a few days later I was at school when the teachers told us that Melanie had passed away. I have asked my Mum what she can remember and she also believes that it was at school. I remember observing others crying, I don't remember feeling upset, just my internal chat to myself of asking myself if this is what I was supposed to do, cry when someone dies? I didn't though, I didn't cry, not then. I just watched and observed everybody else. I didn't think at that time about the loss of our friendship, I only remembered all the great laughs we had and was thinking Melanie would be laughing at everyone now… she really did have a wicked sense of humour.

I think it was a few months later when I was walking home from school I saw someone I thought was Melanie. I ran after her calling out her name only for the girl to turn round and I then realised that it wasn't Melanie, and that is when I constructed other thoughts that she was gone and I would never see her again, we would never play and laugh together again.

On reflection, it was strange, though, because as soon as these thoughts were constructed by me I felt fear, pain and sorrow.

I have to say those feelings and thoughts were short lived as another friend came over and distracted me from my thoughts of Melanie and we started to play. I do also reminisce once I was in the bath and I was asking Mum questions about Melanie and I tried to sort of force myself to cry as I thought there was something wrong with me that I hadn't cried, but even now when I think about her the memories of her are so strong of us laughing so much, that outweighs any negative thoughts. That is not to say that as an adult I haven't cried about the loss of our friendship, but I also acknowledge from these childhood memories that I have cried as an adult because Melanie's loss interlinked with other losses I have experienced within my life. She really did live her short life full of laughter and fun; well, with me she did. The only time that I can remember Melanie being scared was when I told her that women can die who are having babies and her Mum was pregnant at that time. Obviously her Mum politely told me that there is a very slim chance and that maybe I need to be careful in the future what I told people. I didn't understand what her Mum was saying or why she was angry, I was just telling my truth of what I had witnessed and observed from life. However I felt upset with myself, and internally told myself that I shouldn't have said anything. I didn't like adults being angry or upset with me.

At this time Mum had started to help her friend out at a local shop down the road from us. Dad wasn't happy that Mum was at work when he would come home and there would be no dinner. Plus the fact that she wasn't getting paid for it, but Mum's argument was that her friend and her husband had helped us when the pit strike was on giving us food, so she felt she needed to pay them back. Plus on reflection Mum has told me that this gave her an opportunity to find herself again and build her confidence up, to become herself rather than just someone's Mum.

Sometime in between these times, all us kids decided to go to Cusworth Hall because it had been snowing and you could sledge down the steep hill. I was excited because I was allowed to go because my older sister and her friend were going. We got some big plastic bags from the shop to climb in and use as a sledge; it was ace, we went so fast down that hill. On our way back exhausted from our day, we waited for a bus. There were lots of people waiting. A man approached us and told us he was an undercover policeman and that some young youths who matched our description had vandalised a pub up the road. We were all frightened. We said it wasn't us and explained where we had been and that we were on our way home. He said he didn't believe us and that he would come back with us to speak with our parents. My heart was beating really fast, what if they didn't believe us? What would happen to us?

This man got on our bus and started to write stuff in a pad, and took details of the bus. When it was our stop we all got off. I had that feeling again, I didn't feel safe. He stopped us on a corner, explaining that this could end now if the two older ones went with him behind the bus stop to show him their toe nails as the vandals had red nail varnish on. My older sister said no, and that she was going home to tell our parents. We all started to cry when he told us that he would sue our parents and we would all be homeless. Our Ella started to walk home, we were all shouting at her to come back, I remember shouting that we are already poor and that I didn't want our parents to lose any more money. My sister wouldn't come back and quick as a flash the guy ran off. The bus would go up and turn around and come back down; he had jumped on that. We all ran home crying, my Dad was home and he rang Mum. They phoned the police, we gave a description and told our story but we never heard any more about it.

A few months after this, Mum and Dad informed us that they were splitting up. There had previously been an incident where I heard Mum and Dad arguing. I never heard them argue a lot before. Mum had been out with Pam from the shop and came upstairs crying; again, I had never seen Mum cry and at the time I was angry with Dad for at that time I believed he had made her cry. I remember hugging Mum on the landing and saying to her that I think they should split up. I recall this thought came from having conversations previously with my friends about other children's Mums and Dads who had divorced and that they had two houses and two lots of Christmas presents; as a child I wanted to experience that. I didn't have any understanding of the emotion connected to separations or the effect it can have on other attachments.

So when they told us that they were splitting up the thought of getting more Christmas presents outweighed any other thoughts. I wasn't initially upset as I now understand that back then I had no understanding into what was really happening, but I did cry when I saw the effect it had on my siblings and my Mum and Dad. Dad wrote 'Roy loves Rita forever' on a record they had liked together and my siblings were crying. At this point my internal conversation was that this was my fault; I started to feel guilty as I was the one who had suggested to Mum that I thought that they should split up. I had started to internalise everyone's pain as I believed that it had been created by me. My thoughts were telling me that I was to blame as I was responsible for putting the idea of separating into Mum's head, just like it was my fault for making Melanie frightened that her Mum might die in childbirth. Plus on reflection, I was at this time developing cognitively so I also questioned what had previously happened to me with regards to the abuse and why it had happened. My conclusion at that time was again it was my fault because I liked him tickling my back, if I had not wanted my back tickling then none of this would have happened. This was the start of me crucifying myself and creating blame.

My perception of Mum and Dad's relationship was very much split into gender roles. Mum's role was to look after us children and the house and Dad's role was to go to work and earn money. I can't remember Dad getting really involved with us as children, it would always be 'wait till your Mum comes home' if we wanted food or to go somewhere, but I can remember thinking that their relationship wasn't what I wanted when I got older, it didn't feel fair. When we would go out on family trips Mum again was the main carer and authority figure and Dad would back Mum up, or Mum would

use Dad as a threatening tool... 'wait till your Dad gets home'. Dad
would very rarely punish us, that was left to Mum. I do remember
all four of us in the bath together and messing around Mum had
told us loads of times to hurry up anyway she sent Dad in. Dad told
us all to scream when he smacked his belt against the bath, Mum's
face was a picture when she came running in.

I remember creating thoughts that the difference between women
and men wasn't fair and believing that women get the raw deal.
How come Dad was able to chill, watch TV and have time with his
pigeons, but I didn't see Mum chilling; well, except when we would
all sit down to watch TV. However, from lots of other life experiences I do perceive now that the defined gender roles never gave
Dad the opportunity to integrate with us children as he believed
that is what should happen within a relationship, plus I believe
upon reflection that his upbringing never gave him the opportunity
to build skills to become independent and to interact with children.
Dad mentioned to me that his parents worked and he had to go to a
neighbour's house, which he hated, so he wanted his children to have
a parent at home. Is this why he believed so much in the defined
gender roles? I remember Grandma was the one who cooked and
was always doing something when GranDad would sit in his chair
and read the newspaper, so did my Dad only see that to believe that
he should have chill time? After all, he was the one working and
'bringing home the bacon'.

Furthermore, I also consider that my Dad made a personal choice
in that he chose to believe in these defined roles but I also consider
that, just like a lot of us, he made choices without self-awareness,
from his experiences as a child, not understanding that becoming
stuck in a defined role would limit his growth and experiences. As
a parent myself and reflecting back to my childhood I observe and
experience the difference of people being stuck in defined gender
roles as missing out on having strong, loving interacting relationships with children. Furthermore on reflection and what I experience now within my interactions with my Dad is that I always

knew deep down (my intuition kept telling me) that he loved me, but this was always questioned by my thoughts because of my experiences within our interactions, our limited interactions and what seemed to me like his lack of interest in us children. I acknowledge now that my Dad struggled to show his love and perceive that his core beliefs limited our interactions or the level of depth. I experience and perceive the older my Dad gets the more he communicates in an open, honest and loving way.

My perception of Mum at this time was that she was open, honest and loving and I think that at this time she believed in the defined gender roles, but I would also sense her frustration when waiting for Dad to finish with his pigeons if we were going somewhere. Or the times that I would watch her doing the house work and Dad chilling, watching racing or football. There always felt like movement with Mum in her answers to my questions, and I felt she gave honest answers back. When they separated I started to believe that they didn't love each other any more and this worried me to think that they could stop loving me. Mum always reassured me that her love would never fade, but those thoughts kept coming back to create more fear.

Chapter 2

Too Much Pain

When my Mum and Dad split up I remember visiting Dad who I could feel was in distress and pain; everything had changed so suddenly, we weren't a family any more. Dad would always ask us about Mum, how she was, what she was up to. The answers that we would give didn't seem to help him feel any better. I felt that guilt again, this is what I had created, my Dad's pain became my pain, I must have thought I could take it away from him. That I was stronger and could cope better with the emotion. We were close to our extended family on my Dad's side, my Grandma, Grandad, Auntie's and Uncle's families. We would see them nearly every week, and we would take in turns to stay at our Auntie's house at weekends and all congregate at Grandma and Grandad's house to catch up with one another. I loved having a big family – even though us cousins would fall out and get jealous of each other, on the whole we all got on really well, I could feel their love for me and I loved them.

After Mum and Dad separated I remember for a while we still saw our extended family but not as regularly, and I remember feeling tension whenever Mum interacted with them. I remember one day being at my Auntie's house. I was nearly nine years old, playing with my cousins when someone, I can't remember who, came into say Grandad Shaw had died, he had an heart attack. Everyone around me was in panic, despair and crying. I can't remember crying just my internal conversation telling me that everything was going to be OK; again I just remember watching everyone else. My relationship with Grandad Shaw was really loving. He was a quiet man, who always gave me cuddles, sweets, and let me get away with things.

My Grandma was a woman who I perceived as strong, vocal and always seemed to have a smile on her face. After Grandad's death more things seemed to change. Things between Mum and Dad got worse and communication was strained. I remember Mum had taken me to a fair. I am not sure why just me, but I can remember only me there. It was late and so Mum took me to Auntie's house. I can't remember their conversation but I was told that I would stay at my Auntie's house and Mum would go back home. I remember lying in bed crying being really scared, feeling sad and in despair that everything was changing and I had no control. I had a sense that my Auntie was really angry with Mum and didn't want her there, I was upset for Mum and worried whether she would be OK or upset and that she would get home OK.

Not long after this incident Mum was asked by Grandma Shaw not to visit her house any more as Dad had a new partner and it wasn't fair on Jane that Mum would still come to bring us children. We were children, so visiting them alone wasn't an option. Even though Dad would have us every other weekend, visits to our extended family came to an abrupt end. On reflection this was a big loss for me, I loved my Grandma, Auntie's and Uncle's families and I felt it was all my fault that they didn't love us any more, that maybe they could see what a nasty person I was, telling my Mum that I thought her and Dad should separate. I would cry in my bed at night thinking and wishing that they would get back together, I would pray to God and promise that from now on I would be a good girl and that I was sorry. I felt scared and didn't have the language to share what I was thinking or feeling, plus frightened that if I did tell everyone it was my fault that they would think bad of me and I was fearful of losing anyone else's love.

Within this time period Dad introduced us to Jane, his new girl-friend. I was excited to meet her but mainly her two children. I remember the night we met her, her children weren't there as they were in bed. I felt a little disappointed but still excited that Dad had a new girlfriend. I remember feeling really scared when we heard voices on the stairs and Jane shot up to throw her slipper at her children for being on the stairs and not in bed. I felt sorry for them and was a little wary of Jane, however that was short lived as at this time she was kind to us and attentive.

Mum had also started dating Barry and eventually he moved in with us and Dad moved in with Jane and her two children. At this time period I was about nearly 10. We children had been doing a sponsored silence for blind people. I recall coming home from a jumble sale we had helped to work on to see a white car outside our house. All us children were excited to see who it was, as back then not many people had cars, so my sister and friends entered our house excitedly with our sweets that we had bought from the shop.

When I entered our living room I knew something seriously was wrong; there was this intense emotion and fear. Mum was sat with a man and a woman and Mum had told our friends that they needed to go and play outside as they needed to talk to me and my sister. I can't remember which one of them asked, but they said that they were police officers and that there had been allegations against my friend's Dad and they wanted to know if he had touched us where we didn't want him to. My sister straight away said no; this knowing was telling me to tell the truth, so I said yes.

Mum asked my sister to go and play and for me to sit down. I could feel the disappointment and the fear Mum was feeling. I didn't dare look at her but I also felt relieved that I had told the truth. I sat there and told my story, the main thing that I was frightened of was telling them was that he used to tickle my back, which I liked so I was going to keep that information to myself, because in my mind at that time I told myself this is why it happened, so surely they would blame me too. I was also frightened of what my Mum would think, would she still love me? Would I lose her like I lost everyone else? Mum has said in previous conversations that I have had with her that she was shocked at how I just told my story as if it was an everyday occurrence. I can remember the police lady reading back to me my story and me thinking at that time, 'wow, that story is about me,' and I thought she was a really good story writer. Afterwards I went out to play with my friends and eat my sweets.

A few days later Mum told us that Tony was still living in his house over the road from us and that the police were gathering evidence so that then he wouldn't be there any more. I felt fearful; what if he hurt Mum or was angry with me? I don't remember this fear staying long with me as Tony was arrested and taken away... not sure how long it was. I remember believing that his daughter, who still lived over the road, did not want to play with me any more and I felt really sad about this as I loved playing with her. I didn't seem to see her any more. What I didn't think about was the effect me telling my story would have on everyone else, just like when I said to Mum about splitting up with Dad or Melanie when I told her that her Mum could die giving birth. Everyone around me started to look and treat me differently. I would catch teachers watching me, you know, when someone is trying to search; Mum seemed sad and distant, Dad seemed sadder than what he already was, my siblings seemed sad and it seemed that we were always fighting now and friends' parents seemed wary of me. I remember thinking this is all my fault and that maybe I shouldn't have told my story, I felt sad and scared too.

A few months later I caught my Mum and older sister talking. I heard that Tony wouldn't be getting done for me. I asked what was happening. Mum explained that Tony was denying what he had done to me because I was really young and he would get a higher sentence and that she didn't want me to have to go through the experience of court, so that meant he wouldn't be getting a sentence for abusing me. I knew that Tony had abused other children and that the ones that did go to the police, he was getting a sentence for. I started to tell myself that people wouldn't and didn't believe me, I knew my Mum did but everyone else wouldn't as he was an adult and the court believed him, that's why he wasn't getting punished for his sexual acts on me. I felt powerless, not seen and in pain and I didn't know how to explain that, how to show or tell people where I was. Tony got 18 months for the abuse and wasn't allowed to come back around where we lived.

As months went on I found a new friend, Cheryl. We became best friends, I felt safe with Cheryl and she was fun to be around. I had also started to help out at the shop where Mum helped her friend Pam and Pam's husband Keith. I loved all the animals and also the responsibility of taking money from the customers. However as time went on I didn't feel safe being with Keith, I started to get that feeling that something was wrong and that I might be in danger when I was around him on my own. I didn't understand why, as Keith taught me lots of things and he was nothing but kind. It was when he was teaching me how to mix dog food when I really didn't feel safe; he would pick me up to get the weighing scales from the top of a shelf. I just thought it was me and that maybe I just didn't trust men. My knowing was telling me that there was something wrong, but my experience of him wasn't showing me anything. It just didn't feel right when he would bring me down from getting the scales, it seemed slow and my body was too close to his, or when he would help me put a sack of dog food on my back he would lean against me.

At this time things became strained at home. Barry, Mum's partner, seemed more distant and became nasty within his interactions with all of us children. I can't remember when it started but he started to call us names, mine was big lips... you know when someone is having fun and when they are not. Barry wasn't being funny, it was said with intent to hurt. I would cry with some of the things he would say and he then would ridicule me for crying, saying I was a baby and a drama queen. I would try so hard not to cry, sometimes I would walk away and cry on my own.

> *On reflection, my experience was teaching me how to hold onto my emotions and not show them. I wasn't safe with him.*

I didn't understand what I had done so wrong, why he didn't seem to like or love me any more. We used to get on so well, he was fun to be around and played with us, now it seemed he would have a favourite and make it known to us other children who his favourite was. Things at this time were also changing when we would visit Dad and Jane. Jane would comment and say we could only visit if we wanted something, or comment nastily about other things. We would come home many times upset and tell Mum, who would get upset and get on the phone to Dad. This only seemed to make it worse, so we would tell Mum not to say anything.

Mum would always encourage us to have family chats around the table where we could all have our time to comment about what we were happy or sad about. Our conversations seemed to always be about Barry, Dad, Jane and obviously the conflict between us children. I was obviously developing more cognitively and questioning why all the adults around me seemed to be angry with me and wanting to hurt me. The loss of my extended family really hurt and I felt alone in all my pain. I tried to talk to my siblings about what we were experiencing but they seemed to be in pain too, and we would most of the time end up falling out or fighting.

I continued to help out at the shop where I learnt so many things about running a shop, plus Keith taught me how to cook as well as many other things. He seemed to trust me and give me responsibility. I would run the shop if he had deliveries to do, and I worked hard; I would help out after school and on a Saturday. I still felt wary being around him at times but still I wasn't sure why. I was soon to find out.

Things had changed at the shop. Pam and Keith had separated and Pam moved out, but they were still friends and Mum continued to help out as well. I think I must have been around thirteen when I had been working after school, Keith shouted me into the back room and told me to sit down, he was sat on the arm of the chair he was telling me to sit on. I remember feeling really nervous and frightened, the same feeling I had when he used to pick me up or move to help me put a sack on my back, but that had not happened for a long time so I didn't put much thought to it. I sat on a chair which was opposite to the door of the shop, he started to praise me and tell me how well I had worked, he also moved to put his hand down my top and feel my breasts, continuing to praise and talk to me as if nothing was happening. I remember saying to myself 'this isn't happening', holding all the emotion I was feeling inside. I was shocked and in disbelief fighting with myself about what I should do. He stopped and carried on chatting. I eventually went back to work, numb.

The days after that incident I kept fighting with myself about whether it was real or not, who could I tell? Who would believe me? I mean, why would this happen again? It's got to be me, what had I done? If I did tell and people did believe me then that would mean Mum would lose her job and we didn't have much money anyway, plus her friendship with Pam, plus Keith was well known within the village. I believed people already thought I was weird so why would they believe me? I always felt that after I told about Tony that people didn't really believe that he had abused me, because he never got done for me. I then thought about how other people might feel. Mum would be devastated, I told myself, how would she cope, how would Dad cope? What would people think of me? They would think that it was my fault as I must have done something. I decided it was safer not to say anything, hoping it wouldn't happen again but also fearful that it would.

It did and it kept happening, each time I would sit there in disbelief, sometimes I would hold the cat on my knee and my arm close to my chest so that he couldn't get his hand down, Keith continued to talk as if nothing was happening. I started to dress in baggy clothes – maybe it was the way that I dressed? Keith noticed and commented that I seem to be wearing big jumpers, I commented that they were comfortable. I got cleverer and I would think of ways to avoid sitting in that chair, like emptying all the shelves near to closing time so that I didn't have time to sit down. I would hide Mum's car keys or Debbie's, another girl who worked there, as they would leave at 5pm which meant I was on my own with him till 6pm. I managed to avoid him quite a few times but other times he would find a way round what I was doing, by coming to help me finish the shelves etc.

I remember the night I was struggling with thinking up excuses, I was frightened because I felt that I was going to get trapped, that he would find a way around my excuses or that I would run out of excuses and have to sit down. Every excuse I gave, he gave an answer back. I had run out of excuses. I remember slowly walking into the backroom. Keith was sat there on the arm of the chair looking really angry. He looked at me and said, 'If you didn't like it you should have just said.' I stood there shocked, my mind racing: what did that mean, what was going to happen now? I just mumbled, 'OK.' He got up and went somewhere leaving me numb, those words ringing in my ears… 'I should have just said that I didn't like it'… why didn't I just say 'don't do that'? That was it, the abuse stopped… just like that. Keith continued to be fine with me. Obviously I was still wary around him and there were times he would comment about sex or my physical look, but he never touched me again.

My thoughts at that time was it had to be me, I must have done something wrong. I should have just told him I didn't like what he was doing, why didn't I just say something? I made a decision that I would never say anything to anyone and just forget that it ever happened. I didn't realise how hard it would be to keep a secret and what effect it would have on me and possibly other people.

Cheryl and I became best of friends and we attached to a group of people, girls and boys who we knocked around with on the park. That was my safe time; I felt relatively safe with Cheryl and the others, we would have a laugh, smoke and just chat. Whenever Cheryl and I weren't together, people would say where is your other half today? Even though I felt safe with my friends I always felt that I wasn't as free as them, to explore and have fun. I had secrets and painful emotion that I couldn't share with anyone and I would most of the time feel I was alone. On reflection I had developed to be on alert for danger, wary of men, wary of adults and I would forward think to keep myself safe, building defences and not allowing anyone in... I didn't realise this at that time, but this also stopped me from living. I would integrate with my friends but a lot of the time I felt like an outsider and that I was just watching them. Times that I was alone walking home I would sing to myself, questioning why within the words of my songs and expressing through my singing that I didn't understand the experiences that had happened to me. A few times people heard me; I remember shutting up and smiling, pretending I was just singing a song. When I sang I felt free, free from the pain and confusion I was feeling, well, I was free for a little while.

There were older guys that we knocked around with on the park and I started to get attention from them, but not sexually to start off with. I remember one guy saying I was going to be a stunner when I got older and break a lot of men's hearts. I remember thinking to myself I didn't want to hurt anyone, I knew emotions hurt as I was hurting, and promised myself that I wouldn't hurt anyone else. The attention from the guys in our group was nice. It felt nice to be wanted from afar but as soon as they tried to get closer I would feel dirty and back away.

At this time I was still trying to understand why I had been abused and I remember watching the news that said sexually abused victims were more likely to become perpetrators and that victims never fully get over what's happened to them, that they were more likely to become mentally ill. I remember thinking to myself, is that who I am going to become? I don't want to hurt anyone else, am I never going to heal? Am I always going to feel dirty and ashamed of what happened to me? I felt like there was no hope, deflated and in a dark hole. I would move to try to talk with my Mum about the abuse of Tony – obviously she didn't know about Keith – and ask her why she thought it had happened. Mum would say they are evil, other people would say that they are evil, newspapers would say they are evil, from this experience I formulated thoughts and questioned myself: what if their evilness was now inside me? What if I had no control over becoming like them? This petrified me and I tried to stop thinking about it, but these thoughts would come back to haunt me.

We had always had a dog called Mick; well, from since I was born. Mum said she had got him when our Ella was 6 weeks old. Mum would tell me stories of when I was about 4 that I would move our bin (the small black ones) to the gate, climb up, unlock it and take off with Mick to school as I really wanted to go as both my sisters went. I was one of the oldest in my year so I missed out in going to nursery. Mum would find Mick sat outside school waiting for me, and me playing inside the school grounds on the playground. As I grew older and experienced all that I had, I would cry to Mick and whisper to him when no one was around all that I was holding back, too frightened to tell anyone else. Mick seemed to listen to me, licking my tears away and I felt comfort from him and safe that I could tell everything to him, feeling that he understood me, and that would love me no matter what I told him or how nasty I was to him.

I was about 13, nearly 14, when Mick had become very poorly; he had a lot of cancerous lumps all over his body. We had the vet out at different times of Mick's life thinking that it might be the end of his life, so at this time when the vet was called I suppose I believed it would never be the end of Mick, that he seemed to have an unlimited life. At this point he was nearly 17 years old. I remember one story that Mum and Dad used to tell us was that Mick one time had come home from wandering off and they had become worried as he had been gone for a few days (those were the days you opened your door and allowed your dog to walk themselves). Mick had come back home, bleeding, and had been in a fight as he had been bitten all over his body. Mum bathed him but he was really ill. Mum had told Dad that he needed to take him to the vets but that Dad needed to ensure he brought him back. The vet advised my Dad that Mick needed to be put to sleep. Dad explained to the vet that he couldn't go home without Mick, as at home were us four children egerly waiting for Mick to come home. The vet gave him medication and Mick came home and made a full recovery… well we all did love him so much, he had no choice but to recover.

The vet came this night and explained to my Mum that Mick was really ill and in pain and needed to be put to sleep. All of us started to cry; well, except for Barry who voiced that he was just a dog. We all said our goodbyes one by one, telling Mick how much we loved him, Mum asked us if we wanted to be there when he was put to sleep, my siblings said no, but I did. I wanted him to know that I was there for him, just like he had been there for me when it had counted, there was no way I was going to let him down when he needed me the most. I stroked Mick and kissed him as the vet injected him and I whispered one last time into his ear, this time it was to say thank you and that I loved and would miss him so much.

As I am reflecting on these memories, tears are streaming down my face and I am sobbing. I don't think at that point in time I really fully understood how important Mick's connection was to me and how much he helped me to express my emotion and thoughts, by just being him.

The vet took Mick away, they never did bill my Mum.

My relationship with my Dad at this time became very distant and we eventually stopped wanting to visit for many reasons. I wanted to spend more time with my friends, but the main reason was that when we did go I felt uncomfortable and upset with how Jane and Dad commented on things back at home. I remember one time Jane and Dad telling me that I was getting a name for myself on the park. That I was being called a slag… I remember screaming inside of myself, "You haven't got a clue who I am, there is no way I will allow any guy to touch me." I felt dirty and ashamed as if I had done something wrong; maybe I was? Maybe I was giving off the wrong message to people? That is why people would think that I was being sexual with lads, I must be doing something wrong.

So where did I learn to internalise, does everyone do it? What I know now is at that time I had created thoughts that I needed to keep the experience of the abuse to myself because I loved my Mum and Dad and I didn't want them to die. I grew up with adults around me that at that time believed, as society did, that you should keep emotional traumas away from your children so it was very rare that I would see adults cry or show painful emotion – well, not connected to their own experiences of life. I would feel other people's emotion and verbalise at times what I was feeling to be told I was wrong, that they were not feeling that way. On reflection most of the time I would only see the emotion connected to them through watching films or sad documentaries, strange though looking back how it seemed OK and acceptable to show anger, frustration and disappointment! I still experience and witness this now within my own connections and society, that nothing has really changed – isn't that what most of us still do now?

I believed I conformed thoughts from my experiences with showing emotion that it is not safe to cry to show painful emotion and I conformed thoughts from observing others that I believed other people could not cope with painful emotion, so I developed to try to keep that kind of emotion to myself. I know now through my training and the theory of psychotherapy that the only way I could do that was to internalise that emotion or only show part of painful emotion to relevant people that I felt safe with. My Mum was the main attachment that I could show a lot of my emotion to, but not all, because some of that painful emotion was connected to our attachment (such as the abuse, divorce and Mum's previous partner) and I was fearful of hurting and upsetting her and other close family and friends. As throughout my life experiences interacting with people, emotion would most of the time come with projection and blame. YOU ARE MAKING ME FEEL... angry, upset, frustrated, disappointed. I am sorry I made YOU feel... so I developed to believe that I had the power to make people feel that way, and I didn't want people to feel pain or be angry.

I acknowledge now that this development was reinforced by all of my life experiences and close attachments, that these experiences taught me so much about how to learn to hide my emotions and find ways to manipulate situations to try to avoid conflict and blame.

Chapter 3

Finding Safety

I continued to go on the park, because these friends offered me safety. I was safe to show most of me to them, just not all of me. It was mainly my deep thinking/knowing, or what I now know as my intuition, that was telling me about my observations of life, that wouldn't be accepted by my friends, they would laugh and tell me I am weird or too deep. So I learnt to keep that part of myself mainly to myself while with friends, or chat and share some with my Mum about what I would see from life and what my intuition would tell me. I acknowledged that with older people I could most of time communicate that way and they would always say that I had an old head on my shoulders, I didn't really understand what they were meaning.

In school I loved drama; I felt excited to pretend to be someone else. I would get frightened to perform in front of others but something would push me to do it. I remember being in school and we had to do a class assembly about drugs, no one had taken responsibility for it and our teacher was in panic because we were supposed to do it within a few days. None of the class seemed interested in performing so I said that I would do it on my own, everyone was shocked which frightened me but their reactions made me more determined to do it on my own. I practised a little bit but decided that I would improvise. I had an idea that I would be in the police station and the audience would be the police that I was talking to, telling a story of my friend who had wanted to try drugs and died. After my performance everyone was coming up to me saying how great my performance was, I remember being really pleased with myself.

I now realise that this medium helped me to express, feel and explore emotions that I was feeling but safely within other characters so no one else could see that these emotions were also connected to me. This medium helped me to release emotion but not to heal.

I was proud of my drama and would want to show my skill to my family, I remember showing a play to Mum and Barry once. After I finished, Barry said to Mum, "See, I told you she was a drama queen and that she makes stuff up, she is a good liar." I remember feeling broken inside, telling myself, Mum will never believe me now when I tell her what Barry says and does. I was crying deep within but I was determined I wasn't going to show him.

As time went on things just kept getting worse. I felt like I was living in a prison being at home. Barry would either not speak to me or growl and pull a face of disgust when I walked into the room he was in. I would walk back out, upset. If I was sat watching TV he would come in and tell me to "fuck off out"; obviously he would never talk to us like that while Mum was around. So, I always felt that I dramatized my experiences when trying to explain to Mum what I was experiencing. I started to feel not listened to and I started to feel unsafe with Mum and within my home, especially if I was alone with Barry. I felt in pain and all alone. I remember trying to communicate to Mum one day what Barry had done and said, but I felt frustrated with my words; they didn't seem to help me to be seen. Mum seemed to no longer see me... why?

On reflection I had started to close down. I had learnt to hide my emotions because I believed that they made me weak. My analysis now is that my emotions weren't seen because I was not showing them within my communication, so I wasn't fully seen. On reflection I acknowledge that before my Mum could always see me, she knew when I would lie, if I was upset, or if there was something wrong, however with Barry she seemed not to be able to see me because I started to shut down.

At this point in time through my interactions with Mum about my experiences of Barry, I started to create thoughts that she didn't care, she didn't love me as much as she loved Barry. I decided that I wouldn't tell her any more as nothing ever changed and he was still verbally abusive to us.

On reflection, this wasn't to help me as there was nowhere else I could communicate what I was experiencing from Barry.

When I moved to tell friends or friend's parents they would say, well, why doesn't she get rid of him? This would hurt me as I loved my Mum and I didn't want people to think that she wasn't a great Mum because she was.

I now believe that maybe my Mum couldn't see me also because she was in pain, pain from the separation, loss, her child being sexually abused and I know she blamed herself for all of it. My analysis is that my Mum didn't have the time or support around her to acknowledge and deal with her own pain of blaming herself. My analysis and intuition tells me that her focus moved to mostly be on us children, being four of us, Barry, work and taking care of a house. That she sacrificed herself, not acknowledging her emotions, taking care of herself, loving herself, that she lost herself and her balance. She couldn't see herself therefore she couldn't see me; this formulation of my analysis will become clear as my story continues.

I started to feel on edge every day to see what mood Barry might be in and try to find ways to avoid him, either staying out with friends or going to my room. I started to write a diary which seemed to help, writing what I was experiencing in there; that was until the day Barry read my diary. He was fuming and started shouting and swearing at me. He had found my diary and wasn't happy because I wrote 'Barry is a fat bastard' in there when I was explaining another incident that had happened with him. Mum come home to me in tears and that was one of the times I saw her have it out with Barry (she didn't believe in showing children adult conflict). She told him that he shouldn't be reading my diary and that maybe he should think about how he interacts with us if he didn't want us to call him names. She also warned him that if his behaviour continues as we grow that we would eventually turn on him. Barry would try to change and for a while he would be OK, then his abusive behaviour would return. It got to the point that I was always frightened, as even when he was nice I became wary as I knew from my previous experiences of him that his moods were like watching a ticking time bomb, just not knowing when it would go off.

I can't remember a lot at school between the age of 13 to 16, other than my painful experiences of Keith, Tony, Barry and my losses going round and round in my head and asking myself why? Plus during this time other sexual incidents happened to me, like one time I was riding my bike up our street to go on my paper round when I heard a letterbox rattle, I looked over a man was stood there naked, touching his penis. My heart was pounding. I did go home afterwards and ring the police, but I never heard anything about what happened. Another time I was babysitting and took the kids to the shops. As we were walking I heard a whistle in the school woods. I looked over; a man just opened his long jacket and was naked. Again I rang the police, but nothing came of it. Our neighbour over the road would always look in our window spying on us, Mum would always say, "Pervs watching, make sure your curtains are closed girls." On my way to college looking out the bus window a man was touching himself driving. I was so shocked and told other passengers, I took his reg and reported him to the police but didn't hear anything else. What I did do, though, was tell myself that there must be something wrong with me for only me to experience all that I have experienced.

In school I attached to a guy called Pete in my class as I felt safe with him. Pete's Mum would try to get us together but Pete didn't seem interested just as much as I wasn't. We just seemed to enjoy each other's company. He always got on with girls as well as guys, and later he came out that he is gay. I had other friends but I would keep my distance and not show all of me. Plus I never attached to one particular group; I would float in and out of them. This didn't go down well with a few of my friends, especially when there were fallouts and I was stuck in the middle. What was good though is that I seemed to be able to see both sides and I would mediate between them trying to diminish conflict. This most of the time worked, but then sometimes didn't, then I would seem to get the blame and I never really had a feeling that I belonged. Other kids tended to leave me alone though as my older sister had a name for herself of being a bully, as she was friends with one of the hardest families in our village, so I recognise now that their abusive behaviour helped me in that other children left me alone, so I managed to avoid conflict. Children would come up to me and say, "I have heard you can look after yourself," and I would reply that I could, I figured it might scare people to leave me alone, which worked for a long time.

Until one day friends had come up to say that this girl was calling me and slagging me off, my response was, "So?" These friends started to question if I was afraid of her, I stood my ground and said I am not afraid of anyone... complete lie, I was afraid of everyone. They wouldn't leave me alone. I started to become frightened that they would see that I was afraid, so I decided I would just go up to this girl and confront her, to show everyone I wasn't afraid and not to mess with me. I was shocked when she wasn't afraid and gave me verbal abuse back, without thinking I lashed out and hit her. I was shocked with myself. I promised myself I wouldn't hurt anyone and here I was, did this mean I was evil? I walked off leaving her and everyone stood there in shock. On reflection because of my behaviour, my real friends became wary of me and other people with the status of being hard started to take notice. I had a couple of girls challenge me in an aggressive tone but I managed to find the courage to stand my ground verbally and avoid conflict. I figured it was better not to show my fear, this seemed to make me feel empowered and again the experiences reinforced my perception that emotion was dangerous.

On reflection I believe I admitted that fear to myself but not to them as I believed they would use my emotions against me (my previous experiences of life). I was afraid that everyone would know I was afraid, and I would then become an easier target for other bullies. I had enough pain to cope with, I didn't want to lose my safety at school. I have been lucky enough to speak with this girl years later at a reunion, she asked why I smacked her and I told her my truth, that I had been sexually and emotionally abused at that time and needed the status of being hard to keep hiding and keep conflict away from me. This girl explained she was in pain too at that time she had lost her Mum, she seemed to understand and forgive me.

There was another experience where I felt that my hard status was under threat, I was out with my sister and her friend and we had been drinking on the streets. We had come across a girl we knew from school; everyone was jealous of her, she was so pretty with lovely blonde hair. My friend dared me to go and smack her, I said no. My friend made reference to the fact that she thought I was afraid. I was worried that if I didn't show her that I wasn't afraid that then she would start to pick on me. Other people that she tells might start to pick on me, I'd never be safe. I went over and this girl said hello, I can't remember what I said, I just punched her and she fell over the wall. This girl started to cry and ask why. I was shocked and disappointed with myself, I was causing her pain, just like I promised myself that I wouldn't, what was happening to me? I quickly and quietly apologised to her and said I was sorry and walked off, my friend was laughing... I was safe, but the guilt that I felt stayed with me. How could I have done that? I am turning evil.

I again have had an opportunity to explain my behaviour to this girl. I was out round town and she saw me, we said hello and she asked me why I smacked her that night. I explained that every-one including me was jealous of her and that I was dared to do it and that I had always regretted my behaviour; again she seemed to understand and forgive me.

Chapter 4

Love and Hate of Men

As I developed into my early adulthood of 16 years old I never felt fully safe to let go and completely explore life, so I watched from afar and learned from others what to do and what not to do. My girlfriends had started to explore sexually with local lads, and would then be called a slag by them. I would get attention but shy away from it through fear of what people would think of me. I would like and want the attention from guys and I explored kissing and heavy petting then my fear would take over and I would back away, so my nickname became cock teaser or padlock knickers. At this time something was telling me that they were trying to encourage me to sleep with them, so this just made me more determined not to. In fact I made a decision that I wouldn't sleep with any of the guys round our village for lots of reasons, I was petrified, I didn't feel that my body was good enough, I also didn't want to be used and I didn't trust men. I didn't like the name cock teaser or padlock knickers but I decided that it was far better than what my friends were being called.

I felt that I became a trophy and that the guys seemed interested with who would get to sleep with me first, this thinking made me build my defences even higher. However, on reflection I also acknowledge that at this time, I told myself that this seemed to give me power which made me feel less fearful of men; the only problem was that it seemed to attract more men to me. I felt empowered that I had a choice of whether I was going to sleep with guys or not, but I struggled with the attention I was getting and I was fearful of being trapped and not knowing how to get out of a situation or being abused again. I believed that if I did sleep with one of them, then I would lose my power and there was no way I wanted to do that as this power made me feel safer.

I was however deeply attracted to a guy in our village from being 13, but he didn't seem interested and would say that I was too young. Then from being 16 I was deeply attracted to another guy. They both seemed more like me, quiet and deep thinkers. My friends would say they were boring but I didn't think so, I thought they were mysterious and I wanted to get to know them more, plus both didn't seem to be interested in me so I suppose I wondered why they were different from the rest of the guys. I became infatuated by them both at different times, wishing that either one would be my hero and save me from all my pain and the situations I was experiencing, you know just like all the fairy tale books tell us. When I moved to let them know that I was interested they didn't seem bothered, I felt rejected. What is wrong with me? I am not good enough and I am different, I am too deep.

This type of thinking was formulated by many of my life experiences but I remember one time we were out in our local pub when one of the guys commented on one of the girls that she was a slag. I looked at him and said, "So what does that make you then, because you have slept with her." It didn't go down very well and he became angry with me, calling me names. I would always seem to comment to protect others by moving to crucify the person who was doing the judging, even though I see now on reflection that this process meant that I was also judging. I always thought and felt that people just seemed to see me as being weird and judgemental if I voiced what I was seeing. I used to tell myself not to bother saying anything, which meant I started to hold back more, but then started to feel even more isolated while being with my friends, plus what I thought about situations would always seem to happen. There are lots of times I have moved away from people, pre-thinking that I would get trapped by being in their company to take drugs or do things that I didn't want to do. I felt that they were somehow stronger than me and this made me fearful so I backed away. Other friends didn't seem to notice this so they stayed within their company, and many friends did get attached to drugs or get into trouble with the wrong crowd. I blamed myself for this though. If only I had shared what I was thinking then maybe they wouldn't have stayed with these people and they wouldn't be in the situation that they were in?

I wasn't experimenting like they were, I was watching and analysing what they were doing and I would move to keep trying to tell them what I could see. Mainly connected with the guys, in what I believed they were doing in order to get what they wanted. My friends didn't seem to like this and their reactions would be of anger, sadness and disappointment so I would take their emotions and crucify myself over and over again. I shouldn't have said anything, they feel shit now because of you.

On reflection I perceived at that time that I must have a gift of witnessing in life what I had already predicted, in that friends were going down a wrong road. I acknowledge now that I started to feel responsible for my friends and this responsibility would encourage me to speak up about what I thought about situations and give my advice, even if it was not wanted, of what they should do. I wouldn't share my feelings though, just my analysis.

My analysis from watching would be that the guys were trying to manipulate the girls in order to get them to sleep with them, by pretending to be interested or pretending they weren't, in order to encourage the girl to like them more, I could also see the girls do this too but it would anger me more that the guys were doing it. I promised myself that I would ensure that I would be the one to spoil the game and tell everyone what I could see, this didn't seem to get me any friends, so at times I would close down again.

On reflection of my experiences of men, I had developed a perception that they were all manipulators and selfish to move to get what they wanted, and once they had got what they wanted they would blame the girls for it. I had developed a love and hate relationship for men; I wanted attention and to feel loved by them but I didn't want to be manipulated or played with. My perception at this time was that they were all the same.

I had developed not to like my body. I realise now that I blamed my body for being abused and my physical looks, so when guys would comment on me being pretty I would say that I wasn't because I didn't want their attention, or I did want attention from them but wanted them to like me for me, not just my physical looks. Most of the time I wouldn't believe them, as to me it would mean that they wanted something from me and alert me to have my guard up. I didn't trust men.

At this time I had stopped working at the shop and started to work as a waitress. I thought I was free from not having to be reminded about being abused, as it would mean I wasn't around Keith. I wouldn't have to see him again. That wasn't the case though, as Mum still worked there and she would comment that Keith was asking about me. I couldn't seem to get rid of him. Plus the neighbour over our road was still spying on us and would get his gun as if he was warning us.

Barry was still verbally abusive but I was out most of the time so I didn't have a lot to do with him, unless he saw me out with friends especially male friends he would stop the car and shout, "Slag, get home now." My friends all knew to be wary of him. I would go home mortified. Even though I was out a lot, it always seemed like he was waiting for us to come back just so he could have a go. My older sisters had started to give Barry verbal abuse back when he started, but I was too frightened plus I didn't want to hurt him, that was until I really had had enough.

My middle sister and I had been out with friends. It was snowing outside and we were starving, so we went home to get some food.

Mum was at work so we decided to cook some burgers. The burgers were nearly ready when Barry walked in with his son, he growled at us, I felt nervous but this wasn't unusual. Barry said, "What the fuck do you think you are doing?" My middle sister commented sarcastically, "What does it look like?" Barry moved with anger and called her names, my sister didn't stand for it though and she verbally responded. I stood there petrified like I was there but wasn't; Barry had moved to grab my sister by her neck and throw her outside into the snow with no coat. I was numb and I remember just moving to sort the burgers out. Barry came in and started on me. I don't remember what he said but I think I called him a fat bastard, I remember watching his fists tighten and him responding angrily, "You what?"

I remember it was like slow motion of me looking at his fist and then moving to look at him straight in his eyes, and I said with so much anger but really calmly, "You do it, but just remember you have to sleep at night, and that's when I will stab you." I was still looking at him straight in his eyes, I wasn't fearful, not in that moment; I was numb but then I saw his fear, this seemed to wake me up out of a trance-like state. I saw his fist unfold and I became more me, more there, more feeling of anger, fear and pain. I moved quickly in shock to go outside. Barry commented after me, I just ignored him and went to my sister. Still in shock, I questioned what had happened to me.

Barry and his son tried to mock us banging on the window eating our burgers while we waited for Mum to come back. I was still in shock, I couldn't believe what had just happened. I couldn't get over that I really meant what I had said to him, that I would stab him, it scared me because I knew that in that moment I had lost control, meant it and I knew I could have and would have done it. Does this mean I am turning evil, just like the papers said? What was happening to me? I didn't feel safe with me, what else could I be capable of, what would others think? I moved to discuss what had happened to my Mum when she arrived home. She didn't seem shocked.

I think her response was, "I told him you would eventually turn on him." Mum had it out with Barry and things carried on as they were, except for that he seemed slightly wary of me and I had started to give back verbally what he was giving me, obviously to a lesser degree as I was still frightened and I really deep down didn't want to hurt him back, but that was changing and I was becoming more angry now.

> *On reflection, I believe the emotion I was feeling at that moment was rage. In that moment I had no recollection of thinking or feeling, like I had no care of what was to happen to me, just for him to know that I could hurt him too and that I would without hesitation. On reflection I acknowledge that in that moment there was no thought process, no feelings, just a build-up and explosion of all the emotions I had experienced within my interactions with him over the years, which I believe formulated into rage. When I was coming out of that state, the individual emotions were all coming back but I also know that in that moment I had no control over my behaviour, I believe because I had limited self-awareness, because I was denying my emotions.*

Things carried on as normal at home and Mum continued to work at the shop. I didn't have to have any dealings with Keith, just to listen to Mum when she would mention the shop and him. I had started to go out drinking with friends and one time, drunk, I opened up to Cheryl about Keith but made her promise not to tell anyone. Cheryl was great and she listened; I felt a release that I had told someone, but I was also worried that she might tell someone else. My friendship with her was deep so that would reassure me that she wouldn't. The guy that I really liked from being 13 had started to show an interest and I remember going back to his house after being out. He started to try to have sex with me, I kept saying no, he would stop and try again. In the end I told him that there was no way I would have sex with him and I walked off. I was so angry he had ignored me the whole of my teenage years, not been interested, and my internal chat to myself was that he thought that because I had really liked him from being young, he would be the first to get to sleep with me. I don't think so. Plus at this time my focus had moved from him to another guy, who again didn't seem interested.

Until one night we had been out and he took me back to his house; things were getting heated sexually and I was prepared to go all the way with him. It was before we had sex that this guy questioned why I had not had sex with anyone else. I was shocked and thought I would just be honest. I told him because I had been abused. This guy obviously on reflection lost all interest sexually, and sort of made an excuse after a while that I needed to go home as his parents were up early. I felt rejected, broken, I shouldn't have told him, I felt dirty, he didn't want me because there's something wrong with me. I tried to ring him a few days later but he wouldn't answer my calls. I became infatuated with him, I wanted to know what he was thinking. I backed off and would see him out with his friends and he would look but I would look away and feel ashamed, I really shouldn't have said anything.

At around this time Cheryl had told me that a young girl (she was a cousin of the guy I nearly slept with) who used to visit me at the shop was still going into there even though I wasn't working there no more. This girl was only about 10 and used to come in looking at the pets, I knew she was this guy's cousin so when she would come in I would get the animals out and question her about her cousin, like what's he up to etc. Cheryl had told me that she saw her inside the shop with Keith. Fear overwhelmed me. It's my fault, I encouraged her to keep coming back by getting the animals out, what if he does to her what he did to me or more? I was in internal conflict, searching for a way to change the situation but without me having to disclose to everyone what happened to me. I couldn't think of a way to get this girl to stop going. I discussed my fears with Cheryl, she suggested telling this guy. That would mean me telling someone else; what if he told others? And this guy who had rejected me, he didn't want me. What else would he think of me? He would see that it was all my fault, see that his cousin wouldn't be in that situation if I had not encouraged her to keep coming back by allowing her to feed and pet the animals. I couldn't tell anyone, I couldn't cope with any more pain. I tried to push it all to the back of my mind, but an image of that little girl kept coming into my mind, guilt would overwhelm me.

I can't remember how long after it was that I decided I was going to tell this guy, but I did also wish that he would save me. Maybe he would want to protect me and encourage me to tell others and support me? We had been out and I think I said that I needed to speak with him, I remember him walking me home, thinking how am I going to approach this, how am I going to be able to explain, my heart pounding. I think I just said that I have heard that his cousin goes to the shop and that he should stop her from going as Keith was one of my abusers. I didn't cry, I was numb, and deep within, frightened. This guy grabbed me and hugged me. It felt so nice to be in his arms, I kissed him, he kissed me back. I think I said I didn't want anyone else to know, he said he will sort it. He walked away. I felt relieved but also petrified, what was going to happen now?

I didn't hear anything. I was in distress about what was happening, I tried to ring him, his Dad would answer and say he wasn't there or make other excuses up. Didn't he believe me? Why wouldn't he tell me what was happening? What if he didn't believe me and his cousin was still going? For days I couldn't concentrate, crucifying myself again and again. He thinks that you have made it all up so that you can get close to him. He thinks that you are a nutter. One night not long after I told this guy, I was in bed crying deeply at the situation writing in my diary. I have to tell, I need to tell my Mum, I wrote. It was late and Mum was asleep, I walked into her bedroom and woke her up saying I need to tell her something. She was dazed. All I remember is Mum saying, I can't believe it, the bastard. Mum asked what I wanted to do about it, I said I didn't know, I explained the situation with this guy and his cousin and that I just wanted her to stop going. That this guy hadn't come back to tell me what was happening and I was frightened that he didn't believe me. Mum reassured me that she would be OK and that I had told him so it was up to him what he did with that information.

I told Mum that I liked this guy and that I was devastated that he didn't seem to like me back. Mum tried to get me to see that what I had told him would have been a shock for him, that he was young and probably wouldn't know how to cope with it all. That it seemed to her he tried to support me but it was too much for him. I knew it was all getting too much for me. I wanted to curl up into a ball and for the world to open up and swallow me, I wanted it all just to go away. Why was this happening, what had I done for this to happen to me?

The next day Mum asked again what I wanted to do. I said I was considering going to the police but I was worried as it was a few years ago and I didn't know. Mum said she would agree with whatever I wanted to do. Mum had met Dad to tell him what had happened and they both decided to go and confront Keith right at that moment. Mum said she was so angry but wanted to keep her calm and Dad was in shock. They told him what I had told them and Keith said look, I know I have had a bump on the head, but surely I would remember something like that. A year or so before Keith had a really bad cycling accident where he nearly died, and my Mum and Pam, his ex-wife, nursed him back to health. He had lost some of his memory. Mum didn't believe him and said she believed he would use that as an excuse. I decided not to go to the police, I mean who would believe me? Plus maybe he had forgotten, so then he wouldn't do it to anyone else.

Mum had told Pam and Pam's daughter came to visit Mum in floods of tears; he had done it to her as well. This lady was broken, blaming herself for my abuse, if only she had spoken up, she also didn't want to go to the police. I was relieved that it wasn't just me, obviously I had not wanted it to happen to anyone else but felt less alone, and safer that I would be believed. Pam and Mum blamed themselves; they should have picked up on something, why didn't they see? Pam stopped all contact with Keith and the rest of the family and Mum didn't work there any more. As months went on I felt more and more depressed. I needed to get away, I wanted to run away from it all, have a new life.

I would go out on a night out and be dancing on the dance floor and just stop and break down and cry. The girls would gather round me and ask what's the matter. Cheryl would try to protect me and say she is fine, just being silly, come on Shaz. I would internally be shouting I need help, I am lost and in deep pain, it was hard to breathe. There would be other nights where I would get so drunk that I would be kissing guys and teasing them till I knew they were so turned on, then I would look them straight in their eyes and tell them to fuck off, that they have no chance and walk away. The next morning I would crucify myself. What was I doing? I am evil, why would I want to do that? I was so ashamed that I promised myself I would never do it again, but I did and each time the day after I would crucify myself again. I felt completely lost, in a dark hole and I didn't know how to get out. Barry at this time didn't seem to be bothering me. I am unsure if this was the time period he just stopped speaking to me, I think it was for about a year or possibly two that he didn't speak. It wasn't nice but a lot better than what I had experienced from him, so in a way it gave me a rest. I still always felt nervous, but when he growled I started to growl back. When he would stare, I would stare back, when he would swear, I would swear back. My nervousness was still there but so was my anger. I was so angry with men, they were all the same, all would use and abuse in some way. Maybe it was time that I gave that back?

I was nearly 18 and I had heard about working for Butlins. I really wanted to get away, something inside me was urging me to go away. A part of myself was telling me that if my Mum was to die that I would die too, that I needed to support myself. Cheryl said it would be something she would want to experience as well and Mum thought it was a good idea. I spoke with work who said they would take me back when I came back and I packed in drama at college. I was nervous but also excited to start a new beginning, to go where no one knows me, where I could become anyone. I wasn't to understand that no matter where I went, my past would always catch up with me.

Butlins was scary as well as exciting; we worked hard but played hard too. We met so many great people, all of whom had a story to tell. I realised in Butlins that I was lucky. I had a Mum, family and friends that loved me, a lot of these people were alone, no family, or limited family and friends, drama within family and quite a lot had nowhere to call their home, they were homeless, Butlins was their home. I knew no matter what happened I would always have my Mum to go back to. I felt freer, happier and loved being in Butlins. While I was there Mum had had an heart attack, she reassured me that she was OK and that I sounded good being in Butlins and told me to stay and not to come back, she would let me know if she needed me. I wanted to go home, but I also wanted to stay. I acknowledged I was getting better, feeling better about me.

After not long being in Butlins, I had been headhunted to work in Premier Restaurant, the best restaurant in Butlins. This is where some of the celebrities who were performing at Butlins would eat, and obviously customers that paid a lot more money. I was nervous as I knew the manager took drugs; what if he encouraged me to take them or that he wanted something else from me? Turns out that he was gay and his partner was the main manager for all the restaurants in Butlins. Graham and I became a great friends, there always seemed to be drama between him and his partner, always falling out. It wasn't long before I became supervisor.

Cheryl and I got a lot of attention from the guys as soon as we arrived in Butlins, which was nice but I also found scary. It wasn't long that word got around that I was a virgin and I felt that the games had once again begun. I was on defence, trying to work out which guys liked me for me or just wanted to be the first to go there. There was one guy that I liked and he would always show me attention, giving me free drinks as he was a manager of one of the main bars. We would regularly meet up at the end of the night and have a kiss and a cuddle. He had come back to our shed (that's what we called it, a room with two single beds) a couple of times but never tried anything on. I asked him why he never tried anything on, he said because I was too precious and that he had a name for himself in Butlins for sleeping with a lot of girls and that he was not worthy of being my first. This made me more interested and actually I thought that he was worthy. I remember being really merry one night and calling in at his apartment, which just was a bigger shed. I told him I wanted him to be the one who I slept with first, but he wouldn't. We kissed and cuddled but I felt rejected, what was wrong with me, how come all the guys I liked didn't like me? Were they picking up on that there was something wrong with me? Did he just want to be the guy who had said no to the virgin? I didn't want to play these games any more, they hurt. I just wanted someone to love me, to protect me, what was wrong with me?

I made a decision that he would never get another chance, I would never kiss him again, as far as I was concerned he didn't mean anything to me. Not long after, his friend had come up to me and told me that this guy had regretted his decision of not sleeping with me that night, I think my reply was, "Tough." I had moved on; well, I was trying to show everyone else I wasn't bothered, but I still liked him, but there was no way I was going to show him that. There was another guy called Carl who worked in the Premier with me, we had a laugh together and it wasn't long before we became a couple. I wanted to have sex to get it over and done with, I was fed up of feeling like a trophy and searching guys to find out who was playing a game in order to get the title of being the first person who had slept with me. This guy was more of a friend than anything else and so I slept with him. What I didn't expect was to feel so dirty afterwards. I just wanted to get away from him, the experience of it was just that he was having sex with me, I wasn't there. As the days went on I would try to find excuses not to be with him, but sometimes I would and didn't know how to say that I didn't want to have sex with him, so I would. Each time feeling dirtier and dirtier, and eventually I said that I didn't want to be with him. He was devastated. I felt guilty, I shouldn't have slept with him, it's all my fault. I also felt free, I didn't have to hide to avoid him, or have sex when I really didn't want to. Maybe I wasn't meant for a loving relationship?

At this time I had tried speed, a drug that gives you a loving feeling and lots of energy. We used to get it free as a friend went out with the dealer. I remember going out thinking that I wouldn't have a good time if I didn't take it. I voiced my concerns with Cheryl and said that I felt I was getting addicted to it. Cheryl said don't be stupid, you can't get addicted to speed, but I had also noticed that my teeth felt weak and I started to have holes in them, and I decided I wasn't going to take it any more. Cheryl followed me and we stopped taking it. I watched everyone else who carried on seemed to fade away, lose weight, look gaunt in their faces, and have rotting teeth. I remember thinking we were so lucky to have stopped taking it.

I had been promoted to manager of Premier Restaurant, as Graham had split up with his partner and left Butlins. I wanted to earn extra money so I also worked over at a club; it was a nightclub where staff were not allowed in, only to work. I think it was my second time there and we were so busy, there was the guy in a suit that was stood not doing a lot other than directing staff that customers needed serving. This guy was called Steve. He came up to me to say that this lady would like a drink. I was really busy so my reply was, "Then get her one." I smiled and walked away thinking, tosser, could he not see that we are all busy working hard? Steve did go and get this customer a drink. I was busy when another customer asked for another drink, I looked around to see if anyone was free and there was only this suit guy still stood around not doing a lot. Frustrated, I walked up to him and asked him if he would help and go get this customer a drink. He listened and went to get her one, while I carried on serving other customers.

One of the supervisors pulled me over and said, "You do know who that is, don't you?" pointing at Steve. I said, "No, who is he?" The supervisor replied that he was the director of Butlins. I looked at this supervisor and said, "So?" He said, "You can't speak to him like that." I said, "Well, I just did." My thinking was that we are busy and I knew that customers would be served faster if we all mucked in to help each other. I looked over to Steve, who was looking at me and smiling. I thought, well, he doesn't seem bothered, and thought, what's the worst he can do, sack me? After that night, Steve seemed to have a soft spot for me, bantering and commenting that I was a good worker, he would offer me and some of the other staff drinks after our shift. I would refuse, thinking he would want something else. I felt trapped with the last guy, there was no way I would put myself in that position again.

I got offered other shifts at this nightclub and there was a big meeting with all the directors of Butlins throughout the day that I was asked to do an extra shift and serve them. Steve was there and would comment about what a great worker I was. I just thought he was a creep, he would banter with me about my looks and I would respond with short and sharp replies, not caring who was with him. It didn't seem to put him off; he seemed to try harder which frustrated me more to begin with, but after a while, I started to like the attention. I wouldn't say he was a good looking man but not ugly either, dark hair, dark looking and smallish. I liked that he would find my anger, frustration and quick wit funny, he never took offence to what I said to him, I could just be honest with what I was feeling and thinking.

I noticed that he would just come over and visit the Premier Restaurant at different times. I got the sense that he liked me. One afternoon Steve told me that we would have a celebrity eating in our restaurant that evening, this wasn't uncommon but I was never into celebrities and could never, even now, remember their names or who sang what song, unless I knew part of their life story. All the staff were excited though, especially the guys, because this celebrity used to be a big famous boxer. Steve told me that the entertainment manager will bring him over to introduce me to him and that we needed to look after him. I felt frustrated. My thoughts were that he will get the same great service as all the other customers, nothing more and nothing less. I was excited that the entertainment manager was coming as he was really sexy looking, but I didn't have a clue or was bothered about the other guy. The entertainment manager introduced me to this boxer, who looked me up and down and said, "Haven't you got beautiful eyes." My defences went up. I thought, you tosser. I think I just smiled and ignored his comment and said that I would show him to his table.

I went over to one of the other staff and asked them to serve him as I couldn't be doing with his sleazy comments. After a while this boxer called me over. Reluctantly I went; he asked why I wasn't serving him. I explained that I was busy. He went onto say that he was sorry if he caused offence earlier. I looked at him and he did seem genuinely sorry. I relaxed and explained that I get frustrated when guys comment on my looks. We chatted about his life and mine, he ended up being a great guy.

A few weeks later we went out to our staff bar when I saw Steve in there; he was never in there. I went over to say hello, he offered me a drink which I accepted. We stood chatting and I noticed that all the other staff were around us staring and whispering, but I wasn't bothered as I was enjoying his company. At the end of the night we were the last ones in there and he said he would walk me back to my shed. As we got to my apartment, Carl the ex was waiting for me, he saw Steve and shouted at me, "You slag, that's why you finished with me." Steve said he needed to go. I said I was sorry and that I would sort it. Steve quickly scurried away. I was left with Carl hurling abuse at me. I told him to fuck off, that he didn't have a clue as to who I was, he eventually left. I was gutted, I didn't want anyone to think I was a slag, especially Steve.

Not long after this, Cheryl told me she wanted to go back home. I wasn't ready. We had visited home a couple of times while being in

Butlins and nothing had changed. I missed my family and friends but I felt trapped full of all my past emotion when I was back there. Would I dare stay in Butlins on my own? I was nervous but looked around and acknowledged that we had made great friends with other people and I felt more confident within my own company. Cheryl went home and I decided that I was going to stay and that I wanted to travel after to somewhere else. I had been speaking with a girl that lived in Jersey and from what she told me Jersey sounded an amazing place, somewhere that I thought I would love to explore and work. I decided to get a brochure and write to all the hotels explaining my work experience to see if there was any jobs. Not long after I got a letter asking me for a telephone interview with a man called Mr Fern, who owned a hotel. I was excited and also really nervous, could I really do this? I had my telephone interview and I got offered a job applying myself to different roles within the hotel.

I decided I was going home for a couple of weeks then I would fly out, my first time on a plane. Would I be OK? What if something happened? How would I cope? I acknowledge now that throughout all of my fears the one thing that used to help me overcome them was knowing that I always had my Mum to go back to. Mum would always be there, I knew I was really lucky to have her. I left Butlins which was sad, to say goodbye to all of the great people I had met, but I was also excited to meet other people. I went home. I realised how much I missed my Mum, my siblings, and Cheryl. Cheryl had settled into a job and was back with our other friends, she had missed me too and asked if I would stay. Was I doing the right thing? Should I stay? What if anything happened to any of them while I am away? Something else was pushing me to go, which now I realise was my heart telling me that I needed this, that I needed to push myself to be on my own. Whilst back home I still felt all that pain and anger, I needed a break.

Mum and Barry took me to the airport. I was so nervous, but I wasn't going to show my fear especially whilst Barry was there. Mum was really supportive but I also felt her worry for me, especially when we saw the plane; it was a small propeller plane. I ignored my fear and moved to get on the plane. I remember that it wasn't until I got off the plane that I thought, what have I done? All I could see around me were old people. Fear started to creep in; I didn't even know this man. Mr Fern's son was supposed to be picking me up. What if he doesn't turn up? Deep within my thoughts, a tall dark haired guy asked me if my name was Sharon. Mr Fern's son was here. He seemed shy and sensitive, and I started to relax. We chatted a little bit on the way to the hotel, but he seemed more comfortable within his own thoughts.

At the hotel, I was introduced to the rest of the team. There was Karis who I would work with on the reception, and two girls who were similar age to me who worked as maids. Maggie and Kerry were from Leicester. I started to relaxed a little bit more. There were other staff who were friendly and kind but I can't remember their names, they were from Portugal, as well as Mr Fern. I got that strange feeling again when Mr Fern introduced himself, but this time I knew this feeling was telling me to be wary of him. I wasn't sure why but I knew I didn't want to find out. I felt safe with Karis and the girls working there and I soon became great friends with Maggie and Kerry.

I settled into working at the hotel and we all would work hard and play hard. There were comments made by Mr Fern such as, "You would be a different person and could have gone far working here, if those two (meaning Maggie and Kerry) weren't here." I always felt there was a deeper meaning to what he was saying, which scared me, but I would just smile and say, "But they are here." There was a few times Mr Fern threatened Maggie and Kerry with the sack. I thought that I wouldn't stay if they didn't, and I got the feeling Mr Fern knew that as well. Maggie and Kerry were gobby if they weren't happy, people would know about it, whereas I would keep things to myself. We met great people in Jersey and I would move to want to explore sexually with a few guys, always with the intention of wanting to feel loved and protected. I would give in and have sex with them, then feel used when they didn't want more and I would crucify myself for giving myself away too easy. I would move again and repeat the same pattern, wanting to feel loved and protected and move to have sex, then feel used. Why were all men manipulators and just wanting my body?

Maggie had asked me one time to go to the doctors for her as she had unprotected sex and already received the morning after pill. I remember being really nervous but not wanting to disappoint my friend, so I booked an appointment. Not knowing what to expect I explained to the doctor that I needed the morning after pill. He said he needed to ask me some questions, he proceeded to ask when I had sex and some other information, then he asked if I enjoyed having sex. I felt frozen. My internal chat was, this isn't happening, he is a doctor, is this real? I am imagining it. This doctor proceeded to ask me more intense sexual questions. I can't remember answering, I just then remember him saying that he needed to check my breasts. Still numb, I took my top off. It didn't feel right, but I couldn't move; I was frozen.

On reflection, I had developed not to believe in myself. He was more powerful, a doctor, a doctor wouldn't do that, would they?

I walked out with Maggie's slip and told Maggie what just happened, and she confirmed what deep down I knew. He had just abused his authority to gain what? Sexual gratification? I started to crucify myself, there is something wrong with me, there has to be to experience all these people. Maggie said I should report him, my internal chat was who would believe me over a doctor? I am a girl that has just asked for a morning after pill. I felt dirty and ashamed, I just wanted to go home. Why didn't I tell him to stop? Why didn't I just walk out? If I was to report him, someone is bound to say and see that it's my fault anyway. I decided that I would just forget about it.

Not long after this Maggie and I were getting ready for a night out, I had a strange feeling that someone was watching me, I turned round and through the crack of the curtains there was Mr Fern looking, watching me get undressed. I ran to tell Maggie, he scuttled away. Maggie said that she knew he was a perv. How many times had he been watching me? Why was Maggie so OK about it? What about his wife and his children? Didn't he love them, why would he do this? Should I tell? Who would believe me? Telling would destroy his family, all that pain... I wouldn't tell... I couldn't cope with all the drama, everyone else's emotions would be created by me telling. I wouldn't be able to forgive myself, what if I got it wrong? Why are all men sex obsessed and manipulators?

I was angry and I didn't feel safe. Maggie and I had discussed further travel and going home, Kerry had already gone home. We decided on going to Maggie's to meet her family, then she would come to meet my family then we would go to Blackpool for a catch up with friends. The plan then was to go back home and get a job to save to go abroad and work. We left Jersey which I was relieved about and headed home.

Chapter 5

Finding Strength

We did all that we planned and had a great time catching up with everyone, then it was time for me to settle back at home. I was excited being back with Mum, siblings and friends, but anxious about living back with Barry and also being back in my village. What I kept thinking was that it was just for a time period until I had enough money to travel. I settled back at home with ease and Barry seemed fine, still snide comments but they didn't seem to bother me as much. I managed to get a job which I applied for while I was in Jersey at a hotel in Doncaster, it was waitressing and learning other parts of the job. I remember only being there a couple of days when I had a strange feeling that I was there but I wasn't. I told a few other members of staff who looked at me weirdly I didn't know what was happening, but I felt something was.

It wasn't till I got home that Barry told me Mum had been rushed into hospital with an angina attack. I was shocked and scared, what if I lost her? I believed I would lose everything as my Mum was my everything, I knew my Mum kept me grounded, that she was the one person who loved me, obviously other than my siblings but they would fall out with me, manipulate and wind me up. I did it to them too, but with Mum I could relax. I wasn't going to get verbally attacked by her even if I verbally attacked her. She would rarely put me down, I felt safe with her. I was also shocked to what this feeling was that was telling me something. Did I have a gift? Am I just imagining it? No one else talks about these kind of feelings or senses.

Mum came home and she was told that she needed to take things easy. I mentioned to her about my feeling whilst I was working and she said that she gets them as well and explained that she usually gets a good sense about people, or sometimes things that might happen. Mum told me about a time she was washing pots and looked up to see our neighbour's house on fire upstairs, she panicked, looked again and nothing was there. The neighbour's house did set on fire a few months later. I heard about spiritual people who can see your future and asked Mum what she thought. Mum said that she does believe in something but that you need to be careful of who you see because they can send you down the wrong path in life. I felt excited to explore more and asked if Mum knew anyone, she told me her friend Pam had a gift and that Pam and Pam's friend had done Mum and Dad's tarot cards years ago and that they had told them that they would split up and that Dad would remarry. At that time both my parents thought that it was a load of shit, because they were happily married and neither of them could imagine that.

I wanted to experience it and told Mum. She said that she wanted me to be careful and said that if I was to go, then I should go and see a woman she knows. I went and this psychic took a piece of my jewellery that I was wearing and told me that there was an older woman in the spirit world. My Grandma Shaw had passed away a few years earlier; straight away I thought of her. My image of her was that she was always smiling, the lady said what I was imagining and told me that this lady is always smiling... I was shocked... did she just read my mind? Mum's words came into my head: be careful, what they say can send you down the wrong path. I decided that I would just take what she says with a pinch of salt. The psychic told me that I am very close to my Mum and that soon she would be on an operating table but that she would be OK and that I shouldn't worry. I did worry; what was going to happen to my Mum? I can't really remember what else she had said, but I did also feel at ease, I suppose hopeful that there was more than this world. I walked home thinking about another world and wondering what it would look like. I looked up to see a white floating lady near a chimney pot on one of the houses, I looked away, scared, then back and she had gone. I just imagined it, I told myself. There was another incident when I had come home and said to my Mum that I felt strange as if something had happened, our phone rang and my older sister Ella was crying at the other end telling me her car had turned upside down in a ditch and to get Mum. I again at this time put it down to just me being weird.

I wasn't long working at the hotel in Doncaster, when I saw a job working for a new Diner, opening up in Doncaster which wanted a supervisor. I told my oldest sister that I was going to apply for it. My sister at that time didn't believe that I would get the job. I explained to her that I did have experience, I was a supervisor and a manager at Butlins. My sister at that time thought that Butlins wasn't seen as a real job, and my thoughts were: I will show you. I did get the position, and my manager was going to be a woman called Lisa.

Lisa said that she liked me after my interview and that she wanted me as a supervisor. Lisa warned me that when I have my second interview with the area manager, I shouldn't tell him that I wanted to travel more. My internal chat was that I wasn't going to lie. When I did have my interview and the area manager asked me what would stop me from taking off and travelling further, I paused. I didn't want to lie, but I knew that if I said I did want to travel then I wouldn't get the job. So my reply was, "If you always offer me new opportunities then I would want to stay and carry on working for you." Lisa told me off after the interview, as she said she had to persuade the area manager to take me on as he was concerned that I would take off and travel at a later date.

I was so thankful to Lisa for believing in me. I was nervous as I didn't want to let her down and Lisa taught me so much about management, different strategies in leading people and the management of running a diner. My nickname in the diner was Hitler, some of the staff said that my management style was get the job done or get out. Internally this hurt me because I wanted to be able to relax and be friends with the staff at the diner, but I felt when I did, the staff would take the piss and not get on and do the jobs that needed to be done. I felt isolated when they would have a laugh and I wouldn't be included, or arrange a night out and I wouldn't be invited. I told myself it was part of my role and that it was better that I didn't build friendships with any of them as it didn't get the job done.

Socially at this time I had reconnected with Cheryl and some of the other girls from our village, I would see the guy whose cousin went to the shop, but nothing was ever mentioned. I still felt confused and fearful about it all. What if Keith saw me? What if he said something? I would avoid going past the shop and I would try to avoid how I felt about it all. That was until Mum told me that Keith had been in the paper. He had kidnapped his girlfriend and tried to put her in the trunk of his car and that this woman had a daughter. I felt fear: this is my fault, then I felt anger he hasn't forgotten, he was still the same. I need to do something about it, I told myself. I told Mum that I was going to go to the police and tell them what he had done to me. Mum asked me if I was sure. I was. I couldn't live knowing that me not telling my truth could mean others might experience what I had. I wasn't frightened then, I felt empowered; I had made a decision and knew why I was acting upon that. Mum told Pam's daughter, who said she wanted to go as well.

At the police station I still felt empowered, that deep feeling was telling me it was the right thing to do, thoughts of 'what if they don't believe me?' would come, but the thought of someone else experiencing what I had because I hadn't told was a lot stronger and kept me strong to disclose to the police officer. When I saw that he was a man, and a good looking one at that, I was nervous. What would he think of me? Would he believe me? How will I be able to tell him the sexual encounters of what happened? Again these thoughts were short lived as I would again hear my Mum tell me what Keith had done to this woman and that she had a young daughter. I wouldn't forgive myself if I kept quiet, I told myself. I told the officer all that had happened, I remember the officer asking me why I was so calm and Pam's daughter was in so much distress. I just looked at him and said, "This isn't the first time that this has happened to me, I have been sexually abused when I was younger." I can't remember much more, but I remember feeling relieved that it was over.

We had a court date. Mum was worried and asked me if I would be OK if they didn't believe us. I said yes and at that time I knew I would be, because that deep knowing told me that it was more important for me to fight to be seen and believed by people than to hide away, plus that knowing told me I would feel unburdened from me being responsible for what might happen to others. I had fears that kept coming. They will say that I have made it all up and use the past abuse against me, and the defence did... however the defence was soon shut down by the judge and he told the jury to disregard what the defence had said and warned him to stay with this case. Keith stayed with his story of having a really bad accident and that he couldn't remember, but that he would surely remember something like that. After being up on the stand, I remember sitting down and thinking this is like a nightmare, like what you see on TV, asking myself if it was real, am I really here?

The jury came back; the verdict was "Not Guilty". The full jury had to be in agreement with each other to be guilty, so one person could change the whole outcome. I remember looking at the judge as the verdict was read out, he seemed shocked and shook his head, looking down. It was really strange because I was shocked, yet I wasn't. I remember my Mum and Pam were so angry; we came out and I was numb, trying to digest all that had happened. Then that deep knowing came back, my internal chat was I have told my truth, that is all I could do, it was down to our system and the jury to do the rest. I was angry though, I felt it was unfair, how come bad people always seem to get away or receive limited punishment? Whereas the experience of this abuse will probably affect me for the rest of my life. How is that fair, how are our systems fair? Who created them? Are they stupid? Do they not see how unfair it all is? Keith had 12 chances of escaping, we had one chance of winning. Is it only me that can see this? What is wrong with this world?

Looking back, I think because I clung to the fact that I told the truth, this helped me get back into a relatively 'normal' working and socialising life. I say relatively because emotions and thoughts of my experiences would always come back to haunt me at different times. I would cry to my Mum or by myself and then I would be able to move again.

> *How I lived, though, wasn't who I really wanted to be. On reflection I lived in fear, I was fearful of men, of other people's thoughts of me, and fearful what life experiences I might experience in my future.*

I carried on working at the Diner and one day I met the new area manager, Lewis. Lisa had told me he was brilliant to work for. That he was fair but firm and that the owners had head hunted him from another restaurant where they all knew each other. Lewis seemed nice enough and he asked me if I was oriental, I didn't really know what he meant and Lisa picked up on my confusion and said, "No, she is English." Not long after Lisa had told me that Lewis had asked if I would be interested in travelling to different diners to help with the training. I was excited and said that I would love to do that, they said they would start to put things in place.

One day I was busy working serving customers when some guys had come in. I had not taken much notice but when I went over to offer more coffee, one of the guys commented that his mate liked me. I looked at this guy, who had a smile on his face and seemed nervous. I remember thinking he had great eyes, really sparkling. He was sat with a little boy. I felt nervous; how do I get out of this? I asked myself. I can't remember the full conversation but in the end I ended up giving him my number. I figured it was a fast way to get away from the attention and hoping he wouldn't ring.

This guy did ring, and asked me out on a date, I was frightened, he was quite a bit older than me. Then there was the image of his eyes, they seemed kind and understanding. I thought I might as well go and see, so we met. His name was Rick. I was really nervous and frightened which I tried not to show; he seemed friendly, open, honest and fun which helped me to relax. I remember liking him, feeling comfortable with him, but from what he had told me, he had experienced a lot more than me as in sexual relationships and this made me frightened. My internal chat was that he was going to expect sex from me. I know that I had already had sex with guys before but it was when I was drunk, it seemed OK then. At that time I couldn't imagine me to have sex being sober. To have a real relationship scared me for some reason, I couldn't ever see myself in a loving happy relationship. I hoped I would but I couldn't imagine it being real, so I decided that I wouldn't see him again, then I wouldn't have to ever be in that situation.

I did go on to travel with the Diner's and help new diners training the staff, the experience and the people were great. Afterwards I settled back at Doncaster for a while, but I became restless and wanted to run my own diner. Within this time Maggie had phoned to say that she had nearly got enough money to carry on travelling. I had not saved as much and my thinking was changing, as Lewis had mentioned that there might be an opportunity for me to run my own diner but it would mean me relocating, which excited me. Eventually the opportunity came where I could run a diner in Birmingham. I phoned Maggie to explain that my plans had changed and that this was an opportunity that I wasn't prepared to walk away from. We promised that we would keep in contact and we did for a little while, but then contact became nonexistent.

I moved to Birmingham to take over the diner there. I was nervous and excited. Fears would come, such as will I be OK away from home? Will everyone else be OK? Will I succeed? What happens if I fail? On reflection, what always helped me move from my fear was that I could always go back home. I would always have my

Mum, plus the excitement of something new helped me overcome those fears. I managed to eventually find a flat with the help of one of my staff and I settled into putting all my energy into turning the Diner around. Staff needed re-training on service and product knowledge, and the Diner needed a good clean. It was hard though; it became apparent to me that the staff that I had didn't appreciate a 19-year-old being in charge. I tried to befriend them, to work with them, to see what I was asking of them I would do myself. As time went on it became more apparent to me that one of the staff, Dinah, who had helped me get my flat and took me to meet her family at her family event, didn't like me being in charge. Dinah had started to refuse to do the things I asked her to do, saying do it yourself. I thought this is because we had become friends; I phoned Lisa to ask advice, telling her my experiences.

Lisa said she thought Dinah was jealous that I was in charge and not her, that she had befriended me to manipulate me so that really she would be underhandedly be in charge. I didn't want to hear it. Dinah wouldn't do that, I would know if someone was trying to manipulate me. As time went on things got worse and other staff followed suit, service was shocking and staff would always ring in sick. I was working from 6am till 11pm. I decided that the best action would be to have a team meeting so everyone could have the opportunity to air their concerns and grievances. I told Lisa, she told me not to, that I should speak to them one to one, that I would be walking into a lion's den. I didn't listen, they wouldn't be like that, I knew my staff better than Lisa.

At the meeting I explained what it was about and for. I explained what I noticed was happening in the diner, and staff ringing in sick. That I wanted to know why people didn't seem happy. Dinah started saying I was a liar and that the Diner had gone downhill since I arrived, that my management style was shocking and that I was lazy. A couple of others who were friends with Dinah jumped in to say other things, I went numb, why did I miss this? Why didn't I listen to Lisa? Am I that crap? I looked at some other staff who looked nervous and uncomfortable. I could feel myself getting upset when Dinah said, "Well, I am telling you now, you won't be here for long." I looked at her in disbelief and my internal thought was: who does she think she is? I was angry, am I going to allow this woman destroy everything I had been trying to build? No I wasn't. I responded with, "Listen guys, I am only going to tell you once, I am going to be here for a very long time, so if any of you don't like that you know where the door is, and I suggest you walk out of it now." With that half my team left. I was shocked and upset but I held it in. Other staff said Dinah had been saying things about me for ages behind my back. They seemed to feel sorry for me which made me want to cry, so I just said I would sort it and see them all tomorrow. Once they had all gone, I phoned Lisa, crying down the phone, "You were right." I went onto explain the whole story. Lisa was brilliant. She listened and suggested things for me to do, she believed I could still turn it all around and I started to believe that too.

Dinah came back and said she wasn't leaving, that she wouldn't give me the satisfaction of walking out. I phoned Lisa for advice and she told me that I need to log all that was happening and stick within protocol of being on the right side of the law. That this was a personal issue, and that we couldn't sack her if her work was up to standard. I explained all the things she was refusing to do. Lisa said that I needed to log it all and proceed with warnings and re-training. I was confused. Why did Dinah want to hurt me or seem to destroy me? What had I done that was so wrong? I must have done something. Everybody seems to want to hurt me, the abuse, Barry, there has to be something wrong with me.

I decided I was going to work with her and find out what I had done wrong. It didn't seem to matter what I said or where I moved to, Dinah didn't seem to want to cooperate with me. I spoke to Lewis, and told him the story. His response was, why is she still here? I explained I wanted to work with her and work through our grievances. Lewis told me that this is a business and that Dinah was affecting staff, service, management and therefore sales. That what

I needed to do was to proceed with warnings, verbal, written etc otherwise it will be me looking for another job. I was upset and torn; I felt I couldn't do right for doing wrong. I proceeded with warnings, but Dinah went off on long term sick. Dinah tried to sue the Diner for me being racist. Was I racist? Did I say something that was? I reflected back to all the times we chatted, the times she took me to see her family, my interactions with her family. I was confused because I didn't really understand what she meant by me being racist. I managed to get loads more staff in and we turned the Diner around so that it was achieving great sales and offering great customer service. I have to say I was frightened of hiring any other black people, because what if I was racist, and it happened again? A big part of me always wished that I had more understanding, that I could have fixed the situation somehow. I really did liked Dinah, we had got on so well at the start.

Lewis was impressed with the turnaround of the diner and offered me a troubleshooting job, where I would visit a problematic diner and re-train management and staff to help them turn the diner around. I was excited to start something new. My diner would be looked after by my staff.

My first diner was in Weston-super-Mare. Lewis was taking me down. I was nervous, this would mean I would be in the car with him for 8 hours, what would we talk about? I didn't have any strange feelings with Lewis, but he was still a man. He put me at ease and started conversations, he seemed to be interested in why I liked travelling with being so young. I felt like he was searching, wanting to know my deeper secrets, no way would I let him in. We managed to get to the Diner where staff had been left on their own as the manager had walked out. I proceeded to help out in the diner while Lewis went to ring the manager to find out what was happening.

We managed to get back to hotel before the bar closed and Lewis asked if I would like a drink, I said yes. As we chatted I started to sense that Lewis was flirting with me, which made me nervous;

how would I manage if he tried anything on? As we went back to
our rooms, Lewis said that I could come back to his for a night cap.
I was so shocked and frightened but managed to say, "No thanks."
He smiled and said, "OK then." I was relieved when he went into
his room, but also confused to why he seemed OK that I said no. I
started to think about him and wondered what it would be like to
have sex with him, he did have something about him that I found
quite sexy.

Next day we were straight back at work, nothing was mentioned
about last night and we both got on with what we had to do. That
night we went for dinner and drinks, I felt really grown up with
a man who was old enough to be my Dad. I also felt disappointed
that Lewis had not shown me any attention all day or mentioned
last night. I started to flirt a little, he seemed to be interested then
I got scared and backed off, did I really want this? I wanted to flirt
but did I want to have sex with him? If I flirted then I would have to
have sex with him because if he got turned on it would be my fault,
I told myself. The same thing happened the next day and at night we
had dinner and drinks the conversations were easy and I enjoyed
having real adult conversations with him, I knew I was learning a
lot from him.

Our conversation turned to sex. I was feeling turned on and I
started to flirt. Lewis asked if he could enter his finger in me right
there at the dinner table. I was shocked, did I want this? What had I
got myself into? I said yes. I think a part of me wanted to experience
it but another part was petrified about what would happen if I said
no. Would he then want to have sex with me? How would I get away
if I didn't want to? It felt not real, like I was there but not when he
entered his finger inside me, he just smiled and didn't say anything.
Afterwards we went back to the hotel and Lewis went to his room
and I went to mine. He didn't want to have sex with me, I was disappointed. Was it something I said? Did I not feel good? What was
happening and what was I doing?

The next day Lewis left and I was left on my own to sort out the Diner. Afterwards he brought me back up to Birmingham and said he was staying over as it would be late. I had been thinking a lot about him over the week and I felt that I really wanted to feel loved by him and experience him being inside me, but I was nervous. Lewis ended up staying over at my flat and we ended up having sex. I can't really remember it as I think I was that nervous I switched off and just went with the motion. Afterwards he left, there was no conversation about meeting up again and I started to feel dirty, What was I doing? He was my boss. He was old enough to be my Dad. Lewis didn't phone or arrange anything else with me, he has used you for sex, my internal voice said, he doesn't care about you. I felt used, and angry; fucking men, they are all after what they can get. It's my own fault, I shouldn't have had sex with him, he doesn't want me, I am not good enough.

I couldn't get Lewis out of my mind and I would try to flirt with him when on the phone, but he didn't seem interested. I imagined him taking me out on a date and making love in a hotel, that he wanted to know how my day had been and what I was thinking about. It wasn't happening though and that deep inner voice was telling me he just wanted sex, but why would he seem so interested in making conversation with me? Seemed so interested in what I had to say? He does like me. Is he just frightened because he is my boss?

I left the Birmingham diner to troubleshoot other diners, it was sad to leave what my team and I had built but I was excited to help improve other diners. I was troubleshooting for a good few months. Lewis and I had another sexual encounter within this time and I went through the same thinking and emotions until I decided that enough was enough and I wouldn't do this any more. I decided I wasn't going to be used and that I was going to leave, I was angry with him and myself. I was also fed up of living in hotels and being alone. I had been thinking about travelling some more so I decided I was going to go to Guernsey this time instead of Jersey. I went home to see everyone for a couple of weeks and managed to find a job in a cafe and hotel, the owner would pick me up from the airport.

I got to Guernsey and it was dark and raining. There was no sign of the owner so I made my way to the cafe that he owned. They told me that he was called out on business. I was fuming and it didn't feel right. They directed me to the house where I was supposed to be staying with some other people. When I got there, some girls were in the living room. I introduced myself. The house looked shabby and I could smell gas. I expressed to the girls what I could smell; they told me that it had been like that for weeks and that they told the owner who had said he would sort it but never did. The girls seemed distant but showed me to my bedroom. There was a mattress on the floor and no wardrobes. Everywhere was filthy and run down. I was so upset, I made my decision I was going home the next day, I didn't feel safe. I went to the phone box to ring Mum as I didn't have much money and neither did she, so I rang Lisa. Lisa paid for a flight home and phoned Lewis who gave me my job back. I felt a failure, I shouldn't have gone, all because I was pissed off with Lewis. Why didn't he want me? What is wrong with me?

I went back to covering for other managers while they were on holiday, but I had decided to leave still, I wanted to go back home. I missed my Mum, family and friends. I managed to get a job working for BT selling mobile phones, and this was where I met one of my closest friends, Lucy. She was quirky and fun, we both trained together. I remember it feeling strange though as I was a manager working for the diners, but working for BT I was a staff member. I did miss the status and the power that status brought, I felt a bit down and thought people were going to think that I have failed.

Chapter 6

Pain, Truth and Hope

Moving back home was easier than I thought, especially because my older sister was also back home. She had split with her partner at that time. Barry was still Barry up and down but it seemed easier for me to switch off what he was saying, well most of the time.

> *On reflection, I believe it was easier because I would respond, I would swear back and call him names; this gave me a release from all the emotion I was feeling, but then I would feel guilty. I didn't want to hurt him back.*

I do remember one Christmas Mum had taken our nan away, it was Christmas Eve and my sister and I came home from a night out. We had grown closer since she came home and she disclosed to me that she felt she had lost all her friends and her fashion sense from being with her last partner. I reassured her and said she could come out with me and my friends and that she would figure out what suits her and doesn't with clothes. Thought it was about time I paid her back for sneaking all her clothes when we were younger, as my other sister and I would break into her wardrobe. Ella was the first of us to get a job and have money to buy what she wanted, and she didn't like sharing.

This night our Ella suggested that we should open a Christmas present each. We also let Sam our dog come into the room, which was definitely kind of our Ella as she had asthma. It was a really nice moment, when Barry came home from the pub and walked into the room. He wasn't happy and started to verbally abuse us for having the dog into the room, calling us names. I started to feel upset and commented to our Ella that he always spoils things. I could feel lots of emotion, of pain, fear and tears started to fall, our Ella started to get upset too. We both sat there crying, our Ella started to get angry, and said she wasn't prepared to put up with this much longer. Commenting about all the things Barry had done over the years, I started to feel angry as well, asking myself why he was like this.

Ella moved to go towards Barry and I followed, both of us still crying. I think our Ella said to Barry that she wasn't going to put up with his behaviour no more. He responded aggressively back, my pain came. I cried harder and screamed at him, "Why?" Asking him, what had we done that was so wrong? Ella cried harder too. Now both of us through our tears were asking him to tell us what had we done for him to want to be so horrible to us. Barry was still and seemed shocked, looking at us. It was like in slow motion and he started to cry; I was shocked. Through his tears he said he was sorry. We kept asking why. He proceeded to tell us through his tears that when I was younger and disclosed about the sexual abuse, that he got scared. He was worried that we might say that he had abused us. That he was worried that people would think that of him. So he decided it was better that we hated him rather than liked him.

It made sense to me. Barry had changed after I disclosed about being sexually abused. I was shocked and feeling really sad. We had gone through all that we had because Barry was frightened of what other people thought. I repeated back to him that he was frightened of people thinking that he had abused us, but that he had, just not sexually, but emotionally and mentally abused us all because of his fear. He sat there crying, I felt sorry for him. What had he done to himself, what had he done to us? We talked some more and he said things would change, that he would change and that he was sorry. Ella and I went to bed, both emotionally drained but I felt at peace. I understood why. I was wary still if things would change but I had more of an understanding, most of all I understood that I hadn't done anything wrong.

Barry did try to change just like all the other times, but his behaviour returned. It didn't seem to be as bad as what it used to be when I was a child. On reflection I believe that it was because I was older, I gave back and I had more understanding. I would still wonder why he couldn't or wouldn't change, and I would still crucify myself for attacking him back, when he attacked me. I had become good at picking up on his weak points that I knew would hurt him and I would use them.

> *On reflection now though, I didn't just attack Barry, I would attack anyone who attacked me. I would analyse people, find their weak points and verbalise them to shut people down from attacking me or anyone else I was close to.*

This was with friends, family, and anyone else that wanted to verbally attack me or people who were close to me, or even people that I thought were weaker than the one projecting. I decided that I wasn't going to be the victim any more, and I would protect any other victims. The problem was I didn't like myself for attacking and saying things that I knew would hurt others, but I felt I had no control. Once I would verbally attack I would then attack myself internally, telling myself that I was nasty. Why can't I just keep my opinions to myself? On reflection this was a cycle that that I was trapped in for years.

Ella and I decided to move out and get a flat together; my sister had become one of my closest friends. At this time Lucy and I had been going out a lot together and we both got on so well. Lucy had other friends and sometimes we would all go out together, Cheryl would sometimes come out with us and our Ella's friends from school. I was settled working at BT and we both liked our flat. It was even better that two good looking guys moved into the flat next door, whom we would spy on. We had sisterly fall-outs, usually about me being messy and being too drunk and that our Ella felt responsible for me. I remember when I did go out I would get so drunk, kissing random guys and flirting, in the end telling them they had no chance of getting with me. I would feel empowered at the time, but once sober I would remember some of the night and feel so ashamed of myself. There was a guy we used to see round town who I liked, but there was no way I was going to show him that I liked him. Our Ella's friend verbalised to us all that she liked him. I didn't say anything. I remember thinking: how could she do that, tell people how she felt about someone? There was one night that we was out and he was in the nightclub, I flirted with him and he flirted back. I was coming out of the toilets and he was there. I went over and started to kiss him, and he kissed me back. There were some seats in this area; he sat down and I sat on top of him, I wanted him to want me. Things were getting heated sexually and all of a sudden our Ella's friend came over and started to shout at me. I was drunk but I remember our Ella started to say, "I can't believe you have done that." I felt so ashamed but I wasn't going to show anyone, I said well, I liked him too and this guy didn't like her, so what's the problem?

The girls were not happy with me and neither was I happy with myself, but I wasn't going to admit that to them; what, so they can say it's my own fault, they can ridicule me? No chance. I already knew that it was all my fault that this girl felt upset, but why did I do it? Why did I keep sleeping with men and teasing them, to then not be bothered when they showed an interest, or they ended up not interested in me? Was it because I was evil? I needed to change, I didn't want to do this any more, but it was a cycle that I couldn't seem to break. Until one night. I saw Rick the guy from the diner, he looked great, tall and his eyes were still sparkling. I can't remember how we got talking, I think I probably just went over and kissed him, but he ended up back at our flat, we had sex from what I can remember of it. Sex for me at that time was about teasing a guy and then giving in to allow him to have his wicked way with me. I enjoyed it but I never got any real deep pleasure from it, from any of the guys I had slept with.

I can't remember how I started to date Rick, I assume he suggested meeting again because there would have been no way I would have showed a guy that I was that interested. What, for him to reject me? No way. I was wary of Rick and didn't trust him; my thinking was he would be like all the other guys, who used and abused. After a few dates though I started to see that Rick seemed open and honest, about himself and his past and what he wanted from our connection. I felt at ease with him and I really started to like him. He suggested that we become friends with benefits, that if things work out then great, but if they don't, we go our own way and if we ever become single again for either of us to call each other. I agreed and I promised myself I would never give him a chance to hurt me, that I would never show any of my feelings if I developed any for him. We continued to date. My perception of Rick was that he seemed free, always planning and doing new things. He was open about his feelings and thoughts connected to all aspects of his life, this was amazing to see and I wanted to be able to do that. My thoughts were that he was never going to want me; it wasn't long before he suggested that we break up, but to call each other at a later point in time. I was OK, I thought – well, I knew – it wasn't meant to be, and what he wanted.

At this time the one of the brothers next door, the one I thought was good looking, had started to show an interest in me, smiling and always looking out his window when we would go out. We were out one night when I was dancing and this guy came over to introduce himself. His name was Gareth. We started to dance and were having a great time when this girl came over shouting at him, he went over to talk to her. I couldn't hear what they were saying but she soon went and Gareth came back over to say it was an ex-girlfriend who didn't like him dancing with me. We carried on dancing and one thing led to another and he ended up back at our flat. We started to date. Again I promised myself I wouldn't show that I was interested even if I was, I figured that I would be safer that way from getting hurt.

After a few weeks Gareth commented that he really liked me and wanted us to become a couple. I was wary. He would be my first boyfriend, what if I got hurt? I liked him, he was fun and good looking. I said that I didn't like to put all my eggs in one basket. This didn't stop him: he sent me a letter explaining how he felt, I thought it was sweet and I did really like him but I was frightened. I eventually thought that if he could show his emotions, which meant I could hurt him, then I could open up some more. I did and we became a couple. Sex was sex, though again it was nice but I couldn't seem to relax. I would be worried what he might be thinking. Am I crap? So I would move to always please him.

As time went on I started to have stronger feelings for him and he told me he did too. There was a couple of things that made me have that gut feeling. There was a time that a girl asked me if I was seeing Gareth, I said yes to which she replied, "He beat my sister up." I asked him about it and he told me that it wasn't true and that this girl was jealous. That he did once trash this girl's car because she cheated on him. I thought, well, he has been honest about doing that so it must be a lie, and it seemed that he had learnt from it. We carried on seeing each other and I met his Mum and Dad. Gareth had told me his Dad used to hit his Mum and that they don't get on much. I felt for him; it must have been hard growing up with physical violence, I told myself. I also opened up about my past abuse which made us closer. There was another time that I got called to the police station as Gareth had been in a fight. I went and explained to him that I didn't want to be with a guy who was fighting in town. He apologised and explained that this guy had been at him for years and started on him so he responded. I became more wary of what he was telling me as I acknowledged this gut feeling. Things settled down and we went on holiday together. There was a couple of times Gareth got angry and mardy and became jealous of other guys looking at me, but all in all we had a good time. He had been job hunting and found a job that was going to be taking him to Scarborough and he wanted me to move with him. I was excited: a new start and with a man I really liked. I told our Ella, she moved to try to buy to get her own house.

It was coming up to Christmas and I think we were supposed to be moving early the next year to Scarborough. One night we were in town when I noticed Gareth looking at this blonde haired girl and she looked at him; my gut feeling was back. I questioned myself, is something going off there? No, I am insecure, he is planning on moving with me to Scarborough. I ignored my feelings and thoughts and carried on with the night. A few weeks later Gareth said that he thought we should have a break, that he was unsure if things were working between us. I was shocked: where did this come from? I felt upset, but I wasn't going to show him. I remembered the girl, and as he was going out that night, as he was walking out, I said, "Gareth I am telling you once, if you go out tonight and sleep with anyone else, I will never take you back." He said I was insecure and that he wouldn't do that, an hour or so later he phoned to say he wasn't going out and wanted to talk some more. I had already arranged to go out with Cheryl around my village, he begged me to stay in and talk, so I did.

We said we would try again, but that was short-lived, as a week or so later he tried to explain that he thought it wouldn't work between us because we are from different backgrounds. I was shocked, I asked him to explain. He said, "Well, I am from a middle class background and you are from a working class background." I couldn't believe what I was hearing and I was angry. I asked him if he thought he was better than me, he said no. I said let me tell you now, Gareth, you are not better than me, we all eat and we all shit and we all die. Gareth said he was sorry but it was over, just like that. I was gutted, we had been planning Christmas together and I was supposed to be going to his Christmas works party, we were supposed to be moving together, building a future. I couldn't believe it. Why did I believe him, that he wanted to try again? Why didn't I see what was to come? Why didn't he want to be with me? What is wrong with me? Why do all the guys want to hurt me?

A few days later Ella was in the solicitors to sign for her house, and I was also in town with my other sister Sandy and her children. We had stopped to get something to eat when Ella phoned to say that a girl had come into reception with blonde hair saying to the other lady how excited she was that she was going to Gareth's Christmas party, and that he was faxing the menu through now. This reception lady said to this girl, has he finished with his girlfriend, this girl answered yes. My gut was churning. I said, "It's her." Ella said, "You don't know that." I said, "I do." I went straight to the phone to ring Gareth. I said I can't believe you are taking another girl to the Christmas party. He said what you on about, I said I know you are taking that blonde girl to your Christmas party, don't lie to me. His response was he wasn't lying, but even if he was taking someone, it had nothing to do with me as we were now finished, and he put the phone down. I was fuming, I went straight to the solicitors to see for myself. I went in to say to the reception lady that my sister had just been in and lost her purse, hoping that this girl would come down for me to see if it was her. The reception lady came back from upstairs to say there is no purse up there. I then said, "Are you not Gareth's friend's girlfriend?" (Our Ella had already said to me that she thought she recognised the reception lady as one of Gareth's friends' partner.) Her face told me all I needed to know, after a pause she said, "Gareth, errr, Gareth who?" I said, "You know, Gareth Tune." This lady went red and said, "I'm not sure." I said that it didn't matter about the purse, but thanks very much. I walked off shaking. Why didn't I listen to myself when I had that feeling when I saw them look at each other? How long had this been going on for? What had she got that I hadn't? I couldn't believe he said it was about our backgrounds. I went to get our Sandy and told her that I needed to go to Mum's.

I walked into Mum's and broke down. Why did I open up to him? Why does it hurt so much? Mum cuddled me and listened to my story, she said it sounded like he was a dickhead anyway and I was better off without him. I was still angry though; how dare he blame it on my background? I went back to the flat and waited for him to arrive home from work. I rushed downstairs to see him as he walked round the corner to his flat. I said, "Hi," really calmly and asked him if he could thank the girl in the solicitors for me. Gareth said angrily, "Why would I do that?" I said with a smile, "Because now I know what a knob head you are." With that, I walked off to pretend like I was going to the shops. I felt better: I had my opportunity to tell him what I thought of him, and I smiled to myself and walked back to our flat.

Gareth was stood waiting for me. My stomach was churning. Gareth said angrily, "Who do you think you are?" I was still angry and said, "Don't forget I am that girl who has got no class, but I tell you this Gareth, I have more class in my little finger than you have in your whole body." With that I just saw his head; I fell back and put my hands to my nose. I was shocked, he had just headbutted me. Our Ella was shouting and banging on the window, he took off shouting verbal abuse. I can't remember what he said. I went in and phoned the police; our Ella was shocked and was asking if I was OK. I felt OK, I was in shock and my nose hurt but I was OK. We heard shouting from outside. Our Ella said it was Gareth. I went to the window. Our Ella was saying don't go, but I wanted to hear what he had to say and to show him what he had done. Gareth shouted that I better not call the police, I said I had already called them so that he had better take off. Gareth threatened my family that he would hurt them, and said that I didn't know what he was capable of. I was scared but there was no way I was going to show him that. I told him that I wouldn't be scared by his threats and shut the window. Gareth took off and the police came. I told them everything; at this point I was frightened. What if he did hurt my family? I knew he knew some dodgy people. The police said I could press charges, I said I was unsure. I had been down this road before and wasn't believed, would Gareth hurt my family? Would it cause more drama? I couldn't believe this was happening when a few weeks ago we were happy planning Christmas.

I decided on not pressing charges, but I wasn't going to hide away either. I showed everybody my black eyes and busted nose, I even went round town with limited make up on. Everybody was asking me what happened and I told them, Gareth headbutted me. He might get away with court, but he wasn't getting away with other people's disapproval of what he had done. Luckily it wasn't long when our Ella got her house and we moved out and moved further into the village. I had seen Gareth a few times and before we moved he shouted at me and asked to have a look at what he had done. He said he was sorry and that he couldn't believe that he had done it, he started to cry and so did I, and we ended up having sex. It felt right at the time but so wrong afterwards; this guy has physically hit you, my thoughts were shouting at me, but he is sorry, were other thoughts. Gareth said that we should meet at a later point, I said yes and he took our new number. I was in internal conflict, a part of me wanted to try again but my gut was telling me it was wrong, that I couldn't change him.

I told Mum and she told me I was stupid if I got back with him. I knew that deep down, but I felt there was a need for him. I was in internal conflict moving from one thought to the next, yes I was going to try again, then no way was I going back there. Gareth rang, I asked him if he had finished with that girl, he said it was Christmas and wanted to wait till afterwards. That's all I needed to hear. I told Gareth it was over and I wouldn't have him back but good luck with his new girlfriend. I heard verbal abuse as I put the phone down. Gareth rang back and told me he would burn our house down. I don't know where it came from but I said do what you need to do. Afterwards my thoughts were thinking, what if he did? But my gut was saying that he wouldn't. I was scared then I wasn't, I decided that I would always listen to my gut from now on and that I wouldn't open myself up to anyone else again and concluded that all men were bastards.

Except for one: Rick. He had rung a few months before to see if I was single when Gareth was in the room, I had pretended it was my friend Maggie. Gareth picked up that I was lying and confronted me. I explained straight away who it was and that I was frightened to tell him the truth because I didn't want him to get jealous. I think a few months later Rick rang again to see if I was single, I said yes, but I still wasn't over Gareth. Rick took me out for a drink, but I didn't really want to be there, I liked him but I was still thinking about Gareth. I just remember Rick giving me a cuddle at the end of the night. I didn't see him for a while I don't think, but soon enough we started to date again. Rick was his normal, cheery self, and still I perceived him as being free, he worked hard and played hard. I always seemed to be able to talk to him, but there was still no way I would show any of my emotions connected to him, and I started to feel more for him. My thoughts would be that I had no chance, he wasn't going to settle and that all he wanted was friends with benefits. Rick had lots of friends and was very honest that he had other girls who were friends. I started to feel insecure. My thoughts were that I am stupid, that Rick is basically telling me that he is sleeping with other girls. I am not worthy of more than just sex, maybe that's what wrong with me, maybe people know that I am abused goods, I am going to get hurt again. I never got a gut feeling with Rick though, on reflection I wonder if that is why I continued to date him, plus the fact that I really did like him. I felt safe.

After a while Rick said that he felt we should go our separate ways, I was disappointed but I wasn't going to show him. I agreed and afterwards thought, well, I knew what I was getting myself into. I was OK, I didn't feel sad or upset. Maybe I didn't like him as much as I thought? I did think about him and I can remember seeing him out with a girl I knew from school. I never felt jealous, I always thought that I hoped he was happy, that he deserved to find a really nice girl and to be happy. A few months later I was in a nightclub when I saw this girl out, she said hello. I can't remember who said what about Rick but I remember saying he is a great guy, and that it was a shame he had been trapped by those girls who got pregnant to him. This girl's response was, "What children?" I said I was sorry and that I assumed Rick told her, he had children. Why was he honest with me and not her? I felt guilty, I shouldn't have said anything. Why did I say something? I crucified myself. I always open my gob, why can't I just keep things to myself?

From my experiences of Rick I decided that I wanted to be like him, to be honest and open and maybe I was expecting too much from a relationship and that I wanted to take my time in my next relationship. That maybe all I should want is fun, but deep down I wanted to be loved by someone. I wanted to fall in love, to share and experience my life with someone, I wanted to have children. Maybe it wasn't meant to be for me, after all, I am damaged goods. Sometimes I would really wonder, what is the point of this life?

I soon met Darren. We met in the nightclub, he was fun and a cheeky chappy, he gave me his number with his name as Frank written down. I phoned that night knowing I wouldn't have the confidence to call him the next day being sober. Darren thought it was funny that I thought his name was really Frank and told me when he rang back. We started to date. I loved his banter and we always had a laugh when we went out dancing. I started to open up to him about my past and Darren opened up to me too; sex was different, slower and more sensual and I experienced my first pleasurable experience with him. It wasn't just about his gratification, he seemed to be bothered about me. I was starting to fall in love with him. Then after being with each other for about eight months we were out and I felt that churning feeling again. Darren was talking to some girls. I was watching him, my friend Lucy asked what I was doing. Lucy said that I had said drunkenly, "Watching and waiting." That night we had a bit of a barney in the cab home about the girls and the next morning Darren made love to me and dropped me off home. Darren rang a few hours later to say he wasn't coming over and that he thought things were not working out. I was so upset, I was shocked, I shouldn't have said anything about those girls, maybe I got it all wrong. I asked him why. He said he didn't want to discuss it but that I had told his friend something. I asked what I had said, he said that it didn't matter but it was over. I was shocked. What had I done now? What is wrong with me? Why had he made love to me knowing it was over? I felt used and angry.

Chapter 7

Release and Reflection

I couldn't settle my heart was in my mouth. I was in distress. What had I done? All emotions and thoughts connected with my past, the abuse, Barry and the guy whose cousin went to the shop came back. I couldn't cope, I couldn't stop crying. I couldn't seem to understand this life, I wanted to know what I had done that was so wrong. Then other thoughts were, why was I crying over a dickhead who wouldn't communicate with me? But I couldn't stop. My stomach was churning and I knew it was telling me there was more to it, but how could I find out? I decided I needed to know. I waited outside his house hoping to find answers. After a few nights of waiting to see if there was more, I gave up. At this time our Ella had started to see this guy, and he had commented to our Ella that he had seen Darren arm in arm with this girl walking down a street. Ella told me. It hit me, I knew there was more; this didn't give me much comfort though, I just crucified myself more. What an idiot I am, it's happened again, I can't be worthy of a relationship. I still needed to know for sure. I rang Darren, I told him that he'd been seen, I heard mumbling in the background. I said, "She is there with you, isn't she?" He said he needed to go. I cried and cried and cried. It seemed to take forever for me to get over him, I seemed to be in distress for weeks.

On reflection it wasn't just the pain of the ending of this relationship that I was experiencing, it was all the pain from my past experiences. I really don't know how I functioned.

I saw Darren out at Christmas and he went to come over to me, I shook my head and said I don't think so and walked off. Part of me so wanted to talk to him, but something inside wouldn't let me. I would never take him back, my gut was telling me he would want to come back, but there was no way I would have him back. I could never forgive him, he knew my experiences and my past but still choose to go behind my back and be dishonest.

After about four months Rick called to see if I was single, and we started to date again. I was now 24. At this point in time I had just started to work for a stationery company as a sales represenative and moved into my own house. Rick was great with giving me advice and we always seemed to have a laugh. I can't remember sex with him but I know that at that time my perception was that is all it was, I couldn't give more to him. I wanted to but I was afraid he would hurt me, so I wouldn't show or disclose any of my emotions towards him. He didn't want that anyway, I thought he had a good idea of what he wanted and I obviously wasn't what he wanted long term. This didn't stop me from starting to fall in love with him, I found it hard to hold these emotions and felt resentful that all he wanted me for was sex, even though I knew it was my choice to connect with him in that way.

A couple of years before, when I was 22, I had decided I wanted to give support to a child who was in our care system. I had reflected on my development and I acknowledged that I was where I was because I had an amazing Mum who loved and supported me through all that I had experienced. I trained to become an Independent Visitor where you befriend a child in care, offering my time for the child to choose where they wanted to go. I met Sandy, a 14-year-old girl who had no contact with her family. She was living with foster carers who had other foster children and two children of their own. I was nervous. What if I got things wrong? What if I would do more damage? I didn't want to hurt anyone. I needn't have worried: Sandy and I got on great, we were both nervous but within time we had built a great relationship. I would get frustrated and angry at what

I was witnessing Sandy go through. There was a time I visited and noticed that in the foster family home, there would be a cupboard for the foster children and a cupboard for the foster families' children. In the cupboard for the foster children were Asda crisps, and Walkers for their children. I was shocked, disappointed and frustrated. How can this happen? Why would anyone want to take on children who had probably experienced already too much trauma to abuse them further? Did they not see what they were doing? If I lived there and experienced that, it would tell me I am not worthy. That their children were better than me. I was heartbroken. I asked Sandy if it bothered her, she didn't say much but seemed OK with it. Then there were what they called family nights, where they would sit and have a family meal with their own children and the foster children would eat in the kitchen; the other children seemed fine with this. I wasn't, was it just me? Was I too sensitive? What could I do? If I did say something would I just cause trouble for Sandy? I sat with pondering on it for a while, and then I decided to write a letter and speak with Chris, my co-ordinator. Social services agreed that there should be no difference between the children, and that is what a home is for, to be safe and fair. I explained I was worried and didn't want to cause Sandy any trouble. Chris reassured me that they would have a word with the foster carers and that everything would be OK. I told Sandy and explained why I felt it was necessary for me to disclose what I had witnessed, Sandy seemed fine with this.

Sandy told me after that I was not allowed in the house any more and that I needed to pick her up outside. I was OK with that, but when I told my co-ordinator she said they cannot do that and that they would let the foster carers know this. I explained that I was fine with picking Sandy up outside the house, and that I felt that if they forced the foster parents to let me in it would just cause Sandy more trouble, so I asked them not to. I am not sure what they did but I continued to pick Sandy up outside the house. Sandy opened up to me about different things, it would frighten me sometimes as I felt a big responsibility for making sure she made the right decisions. I loved her and wanted her to have an amazing future. I wanted to share my family and friends with her, but social services wouldn't allow you to introduce them to your family. I thought this was stupid, again, is it only me that can see this? Sandy was 14 and mixing with all sorts of people, but she wasn't allowed to come and meet my family, who were amazing and supportive? Obviously, I got at that time that not all independent visitors families are like mine and that my attachment of what I was offering might be different to what other people wanted to offer. I had made a commitment to myself that I would always be in Sandy's life if she wanted me to be, and I would always be there for her if she ever needed me in any way, and I had told Sandy this.

I continued to date Rick. We went out one night on a works do. Jan my friend had moved in with me and started to work as a representative too. I asked Rick to make sure she was OK as she didn't know the team. As the night went on, I saw that Jan and Rick were dancing having a great time. I was so jealous, I stormed over to Rick and said to him that, two can play at that game. I went over to some guys and I started to flirt with them, well I tried, but they didn't seem interested and I felt more angry. I am not prepared for a guy to hurt me again, were my thoughts; Rick and I had a barney. I felt so alone, how come no one wanted me, wanted to love me, what was wrong with me?

One night not long after, Rick and I were about to have sex. I had switched off, felt resentful towards him, I didn't want to be used for sex any more. Rick must have felt that I wasn't there and he couldn't get turned on, he apologised and said that he didn't know what was wrong. I said, "What is wrong, Rick, is that you can't just fuck me, maybe we should just meet up in our late 30s if we are still single and marry." After that drunken night, it wasn't long before Rick said we should call it a day. I was so upset, I managed to hold it in and said OK, but I was angry; here we go again, I thought. I would move to show I wasn't bothered, but this time I was. My connection with him for me was deeper, I felt hurt and I really wanted to hurt him back, but I had not made my feelings known.

I wasn't going to show anyone I was bothered, though, and just told everyone we were friends with benefits and that is all either of us wanted from each other. I hid my tears and put a smile on my face. I think a month later I met a guy on a night out. His name was Adam, he was a good looking guy and we had fun, I liked him and he was a distraction from all my internal pain. I had reflected though my connection with Rick and decided that I wasn't going to hide any more in my next relationship about what I wanted from that connection, as I could see that I was getting hurt either way. I would feel hurt to open up and feel hurt for not being honest and hiding, so either way I couldn't win. I was going to push myself to open up and be honest straight from the start.

Chapter 8

Honesty and Moving On

Adam arranged to come to my house and didn't turn up at the agreed time so I phoned him, but there was no answer. I wasn't prepared to put up with this shit so I arranged to go and see my friend. Adam phoned an hour later and asked where I was, I told him that I am not playing games and that I was at a friend's house and that I suggested that, if he did like me, not to play games and be honest with me. Adam said he was sorry and that he was driving and couldn't answer his phone. I told him he was full of crap and that I wasn't interested. Adam phoned back and said that he was sorry and for me to come and see him. I decided to go.

Not long after, it was our Sandy's wedding. I was still thinking about Rick, he was supposed to be here and I wanted to reconnect with him, so I rang and asked if he would come to our Sandy's wedding with me as Adam didn't know anyone, whereas he did. Rick said that he would come and we had a great day. I remember my intuition telling me he didn't want the same as me, that I needed to let him go. Rick went off and I was OK. I questioned myself: did I love him? I thought I did but how could I if I was OK about not being with him? Everyone was asking me what was going off between us, I just said we were friends with benefits and that is all either of us wanted, and I did believe that at this time because surely if I truly loved him I would be so upset, wouldn't I? My internal chat was that I really wanted Rick to be happy and find love, if it wasn't with me then I was OK with that, I knew he was a great guy and that he had always been honest with me.

Adam seemed smitten with me, which was nice, and I didn't feel afraid with him; I was honest and communicated that I wanted honesty back and what I wanted from a relationship. Adam agreed with me that he wanted the same, it felt easy and fun. Not long after, I was out with Adam and bumped into Rick. I introduced them both to each other; there was a hope that Rick would seem bothered, but he didn't, my thoughts were he isn't interested and doesn't want what I want. Then on another night out with the girls I bumped into Rick again, I was drunk and wanted him to notice me. He seemed to be having a great time and I had lost my friends, I asked Rick if he would make sure I got back home safely and not to lose me. Rick said he would and he gave me his watch to ensure that he would come back. Rick did come back and we got a taxi together. I think I said to Rick that we were better off as friends with benefits and I might have said because I didn't find you that attractive… I am not sure… the taxi ride was hazy, but I feel that it was something I wanted to say to him as I was feeling hurt by his lack of interest in me, and wanting to hurt him in some way.

I left Rick but still having his watch in my hands, the next day Adam came around and saw that a man's watch was on the side. He asked if I slept with anyone, I said no, it was only Rick's and told him that I got lost and Rick made sure I got home OK, that he gave me his watch so that I wouldn't lose him. Adam later that day said that he was worried about Rick to my Mum. My Mum said no, it was just Rick, we had always been friends, he had nothing to worry about there. I was bothered about Rick but my intuition kept saying he did not want the same as me, that he had been honest and I needed to let him go. I decided that Rick was just a friend with benefits and that we had had some great times and it was time to move on. Rick came for his watch and we said goodbye; I let go.

Chapter 9

Building a New Life

Adam and I continued to see each other. I was questioning whether I should be with him or not as he had told me a few lies. One was his age – he said that he was 24 when we met then a month later he confessed that he was 20. I confided in my friend Laura who said, well, don't you like him? I said that I did but it did bother me that he was younger than me. Laura suggested that I should see how things go, so I agreed and plus I thought it was cute that he lied, as he said he felt if he told me at the time he was younger then I wouldn't have gone out with him, which was true, I wouldn't have. Then there were other white lies that he would tell, when I would catch him out he would say sorry that he couldn't help it and was unsure why he did it. There was also the fact that he would ask 'what?' all the time, so whenever I said something I would have to repeat myself over. I pointed it out to him, he said he was nervous that he might misunderstand what I was saying. I felt for him, that he seemed nervous around me.

A few months into our relationship Adam and I went on holiday together and that is when he told me that he loved me. I ignored what he said as we were in a loud and busy pub. I thought, I don't love him so what do I say? The next day he said that last night he had told me that he loved me, I said I knew he did but I didn't want to lie and say that I was in love with him back when I knew that I wasn't in love with him, but that I really liked him. I told him that I would only say that I loved him when I knew for sure. A part of me loved the fact that he was in love with me, but my intuition told me that he wasn't and that he didn't have the qualities that I wanted in a man and that we wouldn't last. I choose to ignore what my intuition was telling me. Here was a guy that loved me, I had always wanted a guy to love and protect me. Adam seemed OK with this and we carried on having a great holiday.

Six months after Adam moved in with me, his Mum said he might as well move his stuff in as he was always at mine anyway. I was shocked to start with, do I want this? But thought, why not? We get on great and have a laugh so why not. Plus on reflection I thought that this was something new, I had never lived with a guy before. We settled into life, working and having fun together, I would sometimes get irritated that Adam didn't seem to want to make decisions and always follow what I wanted to do, but on the other hand it was easy. Sex was sex still, but I felt more comfortable with Adam and communicated what I wanted and didn't want, and Adam seemed willing to listen and learn. I would ask him if there was anything he wanted me to do but he always said that what I do was great. My intuition was telling me otherwise, but again I chose not to listen, I wasn't going to spoil what I had, a guy that seemed to adore me.

Adam moved in and a few months later my friend Jan moved out. I was asked by social services if Sandy could move in with me. Sandy was 16 at this time and had been asked to leave by her foster carers because they were worried she would get pregnant. Social services said Sandy had a placement with a 70-year-old woman but Sandy wasn't using the placement because her boyfriend was too far away and she had nothing in common with this woman. That they had asked Sandy where she would like to live and she said with me. I was worried. What if it didn't work out? It would be like another rejection for her, plus I couldn't afford to keep her. Social services said I would get paid £80 a week for her to stay with me. I felt for Sandy, but was I ready to take this responsibility on? I loved her and wanted her to have a happy safe life, but I was only 24. I thought, where else is she going to go? Where else would she be? Who would take her in? And I thought about all the trauma she had experienced in her life. How lucky I was to have my Mum, who would I have become without her? I shivered at the thought.

I spoke to Adam about it. He had the same fears as me supporting her financially, but said it was up to me. I couldn't see her anywhere else, I didn't want to watch her to be moved around from pillar to post. I wanted her to be happy and safe, I felt that there was only me to care for her and look out for her. I told Sandy that living together would only work if we respect each other, that if she starts to see me as a parent figure it won't work and I would have to ask her to leave as I was only 24 and didn't want that kind of responsibility. Sandy agreed and promised to respect and abide by my house rules, which to be honest wasn't a lot, because I didn't have a clue what I was taking on.

We all settled into life together. Sandy was great. I noticed that she would hide food, so I told her that there was no limit on her eating whatever she wanted and that she didn't need to hide food here. It was like having a younger sister living with me. Sandy was shy to start with but started to come out of her shell more, we would go out together round town, she would get drunk and flirt with guys. Ella would say that I needed to watch her, but I would say leave her, that she needed to get out of her system whatever she needed to, she was safe just flirting. I felt that Sandy was safe. We would have deep chats about life and cry together about different experiences that both of us had experienced but in different ways. I would try to encourage Sandy to get over what she had experienced in the past and encourage her to see what I could, that she is strong and brave, and now that she was older she had more control of her life. I always seemed to give great advice to others but I never seemed to listen to my own advice.

Adam and I continued to date and I had started to love him; on reflection, I don't think I fell in love with him but I did have a deep love for him. There were quite a few issues with having Sandy living with us, mainly not having much time to ourselves, household stuff and that I felt responsible for her. We all muddled through and Adam seemed fine with our arrangement and was adaptable to anything. My family got on really well with Adam and I got on well with his, Sandy would come with us to special family gatherings and in my eyes we were all a family. Sandy had a boyfriend who she had dated since she was 14 and would spend a lot of time with him. There would be drama at times, fallings out, which I found hard work as I would worry about her all the time.

Sandy had been living with us for nearly two years and Adam and I had made plans to move to a bigger house, and asked Sandy if she wanted to come, to which she said yes. There had been different issues at different times with looking after house, running up a phone bill and contacting men on the internet. I had discussed with Sandy how I was feeling and that I was worried that she was seeing me as a mother figure, and this is what I didn't want. Sandy said she would try harder. I was in constant worry for her as she was single and I was concerned with what she might get up to, would she be OK? What if something happened? It would be my fault, I was supposed to be looking after her.

There was a time not long after our conversation that I had come home from a night out to an unlocked door, footprints on my carpet and a photo of Sandy as a child on the table. I was in panicky. Where is she? Who's been in? Who has she met? Has someone taken her? I tried phoning her; there was no answer. I kept leaving messages that I was worried and going to phone the police soon if she didn't ring back, but still no phone call. I phoned the police and explained the situation and who I was, their advice was to wait till morning to see if she returns, if not then to call back. I was so angry, what bloody good was that if she had met a stranger who wasn't who he said he was and took her? I was up most of the night. Sandy phoned next day to say she had stayed out but was fine. I wasn't, though. This experience showed me that I didn't want this responsibility, I was too young. I acknowledged that where Sandy was, she couldn't see why I was worrying. I told Sandy that I wanted her to leave, but that didn't mean I didn't want to be part of her life and that I would still be here for her if she needed me. I tried to explain where I was, that I was young and didn't want this kind of responsibility. I could sense Sandy was upset and I felt guilty. Where is she going to go? Am I doing the right thing? Am I selfish? But I couldn't do it any more, it had all become too much.

We eventually moved and Sandy moved with us while Barnardo's sorted other accommodation out. Sandy moved out and Adam and I started our new life together. There were a few issues that I felt needed addressing, like Adam not thinking for himself. I felt it was always me planning our future, me sorting our finances out, organising the house and supporting us financially while Adam built his business, and he just seemed happy to go to work and go along with everything I had planned. I felt that it was always me that would be going to Adam to say what I was not happy about. I would ask Adam if he wasn't happy about anything, he would just say no, I think we are great. I would start to question myself. Why can't I just be happy? Why do I always have to point out shortfalls to people? Why can't I just accept people the way they are? Why don't I just keep things to myself? Adam is a great guy, caring, fun and really accepting, so why can't I just leave him alone and be happy with him?

Sex was great and I felt comfortable with Adam. I acknowledged that I still felt uneasy within myself when having sex but I was getting better and I would be honest and open about how I felt and why I thought I felt that way, connected to my experience of being sexually abused. The main problem was a lot of the time I did feel like a piece of meat, that I was there for Adam to grab and have sex with, which I really enjoyed but I wanted more, a deeper connection. I would voice how I felt to Adam and explained that I had started to feel on edge when he would kiss me, as I knew that if I kissed him back he would take that as I wanted sex with him, whereas sometimes I just wanted that kiss and a cuddle. Adam would try to acknowledge the way I felt and backed away, but then this behaviour would return; I would feel more frustrated thinking that he wasn't considering me.

I moved to discuss this with my girlfriends. Was this just me, was it because I had been abused? Some of my friends opened up to say that their partners were like it as well, that they would have the same discussions with their partners about sex and being groped all the time. See, it's just part of a new relationship, I told myself, things will change and get better, it's just because he is young. I would also discuss my issues with Adam, my girlfriends would point out that he does a lot of things and that he is a great guy who gets on with everybody. I agreed with them he was, and would do anything I asked him to do. So what if I had to think about everything or organise most things, Adam was happy with that, so why couldn't I be? I decided that I was happy with Adam and that I loved him and would like to commit fully to him and imagined that he would be a great father to any children we would create together.

Adam and I had discussed children and I expressed that I felt ready to start a family. Before we moved I was pregnant, which was not planned and was a shock for both of us. Then while on holiday I ended up having a heavy painful period, the test that I did when we got home said I wasn't pregnant, which we both were disappointed about, and after discussions we both decided to try again. We were expecting for it to take a while to get pregnant, but within a few months I was pregnant. I was shocked; do I really want this? It's too late now, were my thoughts. I voiced my concerns with Adam but he seemed happy and expressed that the only thing he was worried about was if there was ever anything wrong with our children. We reassured each other and we moved to tell family and friends, who all were really supportive. At this time I had become close friends with Sue who I met through working for a stationary company, we were different to each other but got on so well as we both seemed to bounce off each other, we both liked to be honest but in different ways and together we would always have a laugh. Sue's partner

Roger got on really well with Adam and we would spend a lot of time with them after work.

At this point in my life had a great partner, amazing friends of whom most had been friends since we were 18, and a family that loved me and I had great relationships with them all. Occasionally there were fall-outs, but we all moved to try to understand each other and overcome any disagreements. I had still not got a great relationship with my Dad, which I felt sad about, but whenever I visited it just would upset me. I felt that he didn't care as he didn't seem to ask me any questions about me or my life. I felt that Jane didn't really like us so what really was the point? It really was my Mum that would encourage us all to keep visiting, saying he still was our father. Barry seemed still the same but I didn't have to live with him, so it would only be when I went round that he would pull a face that I was there. I would ignore him but it would still upset me inside, I would move to have conversations with my Mum about my past abuse, Dad, the loss of our extended family, experiences with Barry and I admitted to her that I did resent her a little for not getting rid of Barry. Keith still owned and worked in the pet shop which I would drive past when visiting Mum and feel so angry, but I would think to myself that at least one of them had got their comeuppance, as my other abuser had died of a heart attack years ago. I would still wonder, why? Why had it happened? But now strong thoughts would stop me from wondering, thoughts that it was because they were evil.

Chapter 10

New Hope

Adam and I were planning our first baby, we found out that we were having a girl and decided to name her Paris. I would still sometimes catch Adam out telling white lies which would irritate me, and I would always ask him why, but he never seemed to know. I was heavily pregnant and we found out that Paris had a low heart rate. I was worried about what might happen but felt better that the hospital were monitoring me. Adam had arranged to go on a stag do away with friends; it was close to me giving birth, so I wasn't happy about it and I did make my feelings known to Adam. Adam still said he was going, my intuition was telling me that the groom wouldn't go, there had been a few comments that I had picked up on with the groom's girlfriend. I voiced to Adam that I really wouldn't be happy if he was still to go if the groom backed out. Adam said the groom was definitely going. While Adam was away I found out that the groom hadn't gone, I was so mad that I had his bags packed at the door for when he returned. Adam said he was sorry and said it wouldn't happen again. I explained that I didn't want to be with someone who lied and didn't put his family first. I was worried, though; did I really want to bring a child up without her Dad? I knew I could do it, but I wanted to create a happy family with Adam and for our children to grow in a happy family home. I wished for our children to have great relationships with both of us and to know that they were loved and secure. I eventually came around and we continued with our relationship.

I was induced two weeks early with Paris due to her low heart rate. The hospital checked her over and said she was fine to come home with us. I still felt nervous though, I put it down to being a first time Mum. I remember looking at her in the hospital thinking it wasn't real, here I was a Mum. I felt a deep love for her, she was beautiful, with dark hair. When home I found it a shock having a baby; the attachment was intense. I felt worried all the time, what if something happens to her? What if I mess up and am a crap Mum? Everyone was really supportive and we had lots of visitors, but it was after the visitors stopped coming, when I was alone, that I felt down. I found everything hard work, feeding took forever, Paris didn't seem to latch onto my boob – or it was the fact that I wasn't doing it right, as my midwife put it. I felt a shit Mum: I was going to be crap, I didn't enjoy any of motherhood so far, what was wrong with me? Everyone else says that it's amazing, I was tired and really irritable when I would hear Paris cry. I would think, I could just throw you through that window. Then other thoughts would come, what would people think if they could hear me, I am a shit Mum, why would I think like that? I even questioned myself whether I loved her.

I was opening up to our Ella who suggested that maybe I had a bit of postnatal depression. I confided a little in a health visitor who came round to check on us. Paris had lost quite a bit of weight and I explained that she didn't seem to be feeding off my breasts and I was considering putting her on bottle, but I was concerned what the midwife might say and everyone else. This health visitor was brilliant; she said you do what feels right, breast isn't always best for everyone. That was all I needed to hear and I went and got some bottles. Paris settled and started to sleep through from being eight weeks old. Everyone was saying that it was really young, and that I was really lucky. I still didn't feel lucky though, I found it all hard work and didn't enjoy any of it. Adam was doing my head in as I would have to explain to him what to do. I was so tired that one day I told Adam I needed to sleep and he needed to look after Paris, all I heard was Paris crying outside the door of the bedroom. I opened the door to ask Adam what he was doing. His reply was that she was crying and he didn't know what to do with her, I said that I have to learn and so should he… so sort it.

My mood hadn't shifted and Paris was nearly four months old. I was concerned as I felt she breathed funny, really heavily. I told my Mum, who said that I should take her to the doctors if I was concerned, and that Mum too felt she didn't breathe like she should. I went to the doctors who checked her over and said she was fine. He commented that he would be more concerned if she was blue around her lips, and with that I said she does go blue, when she cries. The doctor looked at me. I thought, he thinks that I am this dramatic Mum. With that, Paris started to cry, so I said, "Look." The doctor took a look and said she was slightly blue and that he would send her to hospital for more tests, he had already said he could hear a heart murmur but that was common within babies. I knew what a heart murmur was because as a young child I had one, but as far as I was aware it had closed. I wasn't overly worried, as I just thought Paris would be the same as me. Adam was worried but I reassured him.

Chapter 11

Fear vs Hope

A few weeks later, Paris had had her tests and I had an appointment at the hospital to get the results. A few nights before I had a nightmare that there was something wrong with Paris and I was running up the hospital corridor crying to Adam. I just thought maybe I was more worried than I first thought. Sue my friend came with me to get the results. The consultant from Leeds hospital told me straight away that there was something seriously wrong with our Paris's heart and that I needed to get to Leeds hospital straight away. I was numb, in shock; was this a dream? Was I still dreaming? I looked at him and said what are you are telling me, that she could die? The consultant said yes, that is why we need to get her to Leeds straight away. Sue looked shocked too. We just looked at each other, then I moved to say I needed to ring people. I phoned Adam and started to cry, my dream was coming true, my poor baby. I thought horrible things about her, it was all my fault. I remember looking at myself in the toilet mirror crying, praying within to God that I was sorry, I would promise that from now on I would love her always, please don't take my baby away. Sue was upset and she tried to comfort me, I said to Sue it was my fault, I smoked through my pregnancy, Sue tried to reassure me that everything was going to be OK.

The weeks that followed were a nightmare, they didn't know what was wrong with Paris, they were confused because she was a healthy weight baby whereas all the other babies were underweight. Paris's breathing wasn't very good and they knew that they would need to operate, but all the tests didn't show anything. We had specialists come from different places and still they had no answers. In the end they told us that the surgeon would have to go in blind and give her open heart surgery, that they needed to warn us that if the issue was her lungs then there wouldn't be anything that they could do, as they would be too small. I was in distress. My hair was falling out, Adam couldn't stop crying, what was happening, what had I done that was so wrong in my life to experience all this? What would happen to our beautiful daughter? Life seemed so unfair. What is it all about? What's the point of loving and being kind when all you get back is hurt and pain? There were so many unanswered questions that no one had the answers to, but at present she wasn't in as dangerous a state as other children on the ward so we would have to wait. I think we were in for over a month until there was an operating slot for our Paris. At times I didn't mind, because there were other children that were struggling to live and in distress that needed an operation straight away. We became friends with other parents on the ward and witnessed a lot of pain, where one parent's child died, and hope where other children lived.

Our Paris was still eating and putting weight on, to look at her you wouldn't believe there was an issue, which I think was a blessing and not. A blessing that she wasn't in distress and was developing into a happy smiling baby, but not that we didn't have a clue what we were facing or how it was going to end, plus we had to wait to find out. I was all over the place; some days I would have hope and others I would be in despair. The one thing that kept my hope going was my intuition telling me she would be OK and the fact that before giving birth I had gone to a tarot woman who had said I was having a girl and that she would be a chatterbox. I was thinking, she has to live if she is to talk. This tarot woman told my sister that there would be some distress after the birth and that she would need to support me, but both of us thought that was about me being depressed.

The day of Paris's operation came. We were all lost and worried, and family came up to support us. They would take us out of the hospital while she went under. I went down with her while they put her to sleep, it was unreal, I was heartbroken, my poor baby. Adam was crying and all our family looked a little lost, Mum gave me a cuddle and we all went to a restaurant. I was in two minds, what if we needed to get back? What if she needed us? Everyone said it would do us good rather than be stuck in there, as they said the operation would take about eight hours. I would feel like I was there but not, there would be chatter but I couldn't really make sense of what people were saying, then I could hear them again.

We were still in the restaurant when I got a phone call from the hospital saying we needed to get back straight away, the surgeon wanted to talk to us. I don't think I asked any questions, I just put the phone down and said to everyone we had to go. Adam asked who it was. I explained the hospital and they wanted us back up there, we were all confused and everyone started to ask me questions that I didn't have the answers to; it had only been about four hours. Thoughts started to race through my mind. She is dead, they can't do anything for her. Adam and I started to run. I started to air my concerns that it had only been four hours Adam had them too. We were both in a daze running back to the hospital, voicing our fears and hopes, why hadn't they said anything on the phone? Did that mean it was bad news? It seemed like forever to get there. When we did no one could tell us anything, we had to wait for the surgeon, which again seemed like a lifetime. Adam and I would nearly start to cry, then either one of us would support the other and say to each other that we didn't know yet.

The surgeon walked in. I couldn't read him, he didn't smile, my heart was sinking. Then he said the operation had gone well. What? What is he on about? He proceeded to say that Paris had a small hole between the wall chambers of her heart, and that is why they couldn't detect what was wrong, that he had patched it up and ended up being a simple operation. Was this really happening? It was... our daughter was going to be OK. I felt relieved, it was real, she was OK, it was over.

Months after, there was worry that we weren't looking after her correctly but I wasn't depressed, I appreciated every moment, thanked my lucky stars that she was here. Don't get me wrong, I found being a parent hard work, questioning myself all the time, but Paris was growing into a happy thriving toddler. She had a leaking valve but no further operation would be required and they would just keep an eye on her.

I managed to get into a routine and went back to work, but I acknowledge now that I had started to drink more on a night. Bacardi and diet Coke; it helped me to relax, to stop overthinking things. When Paris was asleep that was my time, to chill, to watch TV, soaps, drama and switch off. Adam would go into the conservatory and play on his games which was fine with me, I had my space and he had his. As time went on I mentioned to Adam that I didn't want just one child and that I wanted another baby. Adam was concerned: what if something else would happen to another child? We spoke with the doctors who told us we had a 5% or 10% chance more than any other person of having another child with a heart problem. We both decided to have another child; Paris was three and healthy when I got pregnant with Jessica.

I would have fears of something being wrong with Jessica, but other thoughts that I would cope anyway from all that I have been through would outweigh them. When I was about six months pregnant they detected a low heart rate in Jessica; at times I was fearful and worried but I knew what to expect and the hospital were aware of our Paris so they kept a closer eye on us. They explained that once Jessica was born she would need to go straight to Leeds hospital. I was OK with that and thought whatever they needed to do to ensure she was OK, plus I knew Leeds staff were great from being there with our Paris. They would leave me to give birth naturally, as long as Jessica's heart rate didn't change.

Closer to my due date I had started to get anxious. I wanted her out so they could see what was wrong, as her heart rate was still low. I aired my concerns and asked if they would induce me like with Paris, they said no. I had a scan two weeks before my due date and they saw that Jessica's heart rate was even lower, they wanted to keep me in to monitor me. I was in the bed for two days. I was becoming more anxious, what were they playing at? Just get her out. I would ask what they were planning on doing, they said just monitoring at present. I told them that I wanted them to get her out, Jessica's heart rate didn't settle so eventually they listened and started the process of inducing me. It wasn't working, I was stuck and becoming more anxious. Jessica's heart rate was fluctuating and going really low. They eventually made the decision to give me a caesarean. I was petrified. I had never had an operation before and was fearful of something going wrong. I told the anaesthetist my fear, he reassured me and said he was there to ensure I was OK and breathing. This reassurance helped me to relax more. I would still panic, thinking that I couldn't swallow, but other thoughts of Jessica and her being safe would help me to calm down.

Jessica was born and I was relieved. She was beautiful and lots of dark hair just like our Paris. They showed me her and whisked her away to check her over. I felt safe that they knew what they were looking for and that she would be OK. I was taken back to the ward and given morphine for the pain, and I relaxed. I was able to see her before they took Jessica to Leeds, and gave her a cuddle and a kiss and told her to be brave and that she would be back with Mummy soon. I was fine when Jessica left as I knew that Leeds would take great care of her, plus my family were visiting Jessica and me. I would phone and speak with the nurses who would tell me how beautiful she was and such a peaceful baby, again you wouldn't believe that there was anything wrong with her. They tested Jessica and found that she had holes in her heart, but wanted to monitor her and allow her to grow to get stronger before operating, that was if they needed to. There was hope that the holes might close on their own, and I clung to that. We were able to bring her home and just keep visiting the hospital and obviously to watch out for any signs of heart failure. I healed quickly, I remember the doctor telling me that here was some tablets and that I should take all of them, not to miss one and that then I wouldn't be in pain, not to do too much, and I would know because I would feel a tug in my stomach. I followed the advice that I was given and listened to my body to direct me if I had done too much, and then I would lay down and rest. I have to say I was surprised with how quickly I healed and recovered without feeling any pain.

It was hard, to know that Jessica had a heart problem and that it wasn't fixed or not to know what might happen, and on reflection what kept me from panicking was listening to my intuition, knowing that I would deal with whatever was to come. Jessica was growing in a healthy way and her low heart rate wasn't causing any issues; the hospital would check her over once a year and if I was concerned then I could call them and they would get her in faster. In the winter I would worry more, as both our girls would catch chest infections and it would take them ages to get over them. They would always be on antibiotics, and managing their health, development, full time work, household management and financial planning was becoming really stressful.

I would sometimes feel so down that I would question the point of continuing with this life; financially we always seemed to be struggling. When I would think 'we are sorted now', something else would happen and we would have no money again. I would get so frustrated with Adam because he didn't seem to have the same mindset as me with regards to money, and seemed to always waste money or not think about how to save, or what we could save on. I was still working as a representative which was getting more stressful, more controlling structures, and Adam was self-employed so we never knew where we were financially with his money. I would point out to him areas where he was wasting money within his company, he would seem to move to change things, then all of a sudden he would make a mistake on a job and the money that we saved was gone, or he would go out and blow £130 on a night out, or want expensive clothes. Adam's argument would be that he works hard so he wants to enjoy things and that he didn't go out much, which he didn't. My argument would be that we can enjoy, but that we would have more enjoyment if we managed our spending and what we chose to spend on. I would feel like I was banging my head against a brick wall. I'd feel even more frustrated when we would visit my sister and her husband as I felt they sided with Adam, and no one seemed to see where I was coming from. I would try to explain, but they would say, well, you are a bit controlling and Adam does work hard, plus that I smoked so they felt I got more money because of this habit. I would explain that I was aware of what money I spent and that's why I would buy cheaper clothes, take my own Bacardi out on nights out, to make it fair. They just didn't seem to get me, Ella sometimes would but not fully, and I'd feel alone and frustrated at not being fully seen.

Chapter 12

Fighting to be Seen

Adam's Mum seemed to see what I did and would comment to Adam all the time that we have what we have because of what I do. I would still question myself, am I controlling? Could Adam have more? He does work hard. Then another part of me would be screaming within, saying I work hard too, I am the one who is working full time, responsible for two children, managing a household and responsible for our financial planning. I would voice what I do to Ella, and she would agree but also tell me, "Sharon, you do have a good man there, Adam always does what you ask of him." I would question myself again. Maybe I am being too hard on him? He does do what I ask of him and he is caring and he does love me. These arguments would come up again and again, when I would feel that Adam didn't get me or didn't seem to want to see me, I would move to try other ways.

I would ask him to take responsibility for our finances, I thought that then he would feel the pressure; he would say no, that I am better at it than him. I would feel somewhat relieved as I did acknowledge at that point I didn't trust him with money. There would be discussions about gender differences and roles that we adopt when we would visit my sisters, and I would get so frustrated at their thinking. The three of them would think it was OK that the guys went to the pub on Christmas Day while me and our Ella cooked Christmas dinner. I would give in and still go to our Ella's on Christmas Day, mainly because I wanted us all to be together. I would sometimes feel attacked for the way I wanted mine and Adam's relationship to be. There would be times when I really had had enough, and I would lash out and tell Adam that if he wants a woman to care for him and do all that he wants, then I am not the woman for him and he better find himself someone else. Then I would feel guilty; well, he does try and he does work hard, would be my thoughts. Maybe I am expecting too much, why can't I just be happy with what I have?

At this time I had built great relationships with my close friends. There were ten of us and we would move to always be there for each other if we needed to download; at this time we were all going through different life changes, with having children and building homes with partners. Fitting time in to see each other was harder due to other commitments in our life. We decided that we would always have a girly night once a month. It started off either at mine or Lucy's, this way it would be cheap for everyone and it would keep us all together. We would chat about everything from kids, men, sex, we would judge each other at times and get frustrated, disappointed, angry, jealous of each other, but eventually we would always talk and work through it.

Then Lucy reflected and suggested it would be fairer if we all had to have a girly night, and that it was up to the host whether they cooked or we got takeaway. If the host cooked then everyone else would bring puddings and drinks, if we got take away then the host would provide puddings and drinks. From reflecting I knew that these girly nights helped me; helped me to see other people have the same struggles as me, helped me feel supported and sometimes not, helped me to feel that I wasn't alone in some of my experiences, even though I felt alone. I acknowledged that I was needing alcohol to help me relax more on a night, I would wake up the next day feeling shit and crucify myself, what am I doing? I shouldn't be drinking, what would other people think and say? I was drinking about four or five times a week, and I felt that what I was doing was wrong, I didn't feel happy, why? I looked at my life. I had a good paid job, loving family and friends and a partner that loved me, I didn't have anything to be miserable about, I would tell myself. Maybe I am selfish? Maybe people would be better off if I wasn't around?

I decided I wasn't fulfilled in my job, It wasn't what I really wanted to do, but what did I really want to do? How could I move? I was stuck, two kids, a big mortgage, I needed the money to survive, to live. One of my friends, Michelle, told me that she thought I would be great as a counsellor whilst chatting about what I wanted to do. I explained that when I was 22 I had applied to study counselling, something I believed I would love, helping others overcome trauma. When I had my interview I was told I was too young and to come back when I had enough life experience, I had said to the woman, you don't know what life experiences I have had and I could have gone through far more life experiences than a 60 year old ever will, she didn't budge and I walked away feeling frustrated. Why don't people listen and understand? I was thinking maybe, when I am older, they might understand me. I remembered being a child and feeling the same frustration, that no one seemed to see me or understand where I was coming from. I remember always wishing I was older as a child, as I perceived people always seemed to listen and understand older people. I have always been aware that I attracted strangers, that people would come up to me when we were on nights out and tell me their life story, people would open up and sometimes cry. Sue and I had been in York on a hen do and we were chatting to some guys when

an older man asked if he could speak to me. I said yes and he explained that he felt he could talk to me for some reason. This guy explained that he was worried because he had had a fight a few weeks ago and the man he punched didn't get up; he was unsure whether he was dead or not. Obviously I was shocked, What was I supposed to do? How could I help him or this other guy? I just listened and said it sounds like he needed to make a decision and to ask himself whether he could live with not knowing what happened, or go to the police and tell the truth. This guy was really thankful. I wondered whether someone was having a joke and looked around, but no one seemed to be with him. There have been lots of other experiences but I always thought it was because I was weird, too deep, that I asked questions which would open people up and that I made them cry by asking them deeper questions. I would tell my experiences to family and friends who would duplicate my fears, well you are a bit deep, sometimes you do make people cry, maybe you shouldn't ask so many questions? I would tell myself that I shouldn't ask people questions, that I was nosy, and that I was making things worse for people.

I was stuck and feeling more and more down. How could I change my life? I was with a colleague one day talking about travelling and I was saying I would love to travel. I couldn't see me doing that now that I have kids, that it would have to wait until the kids were older. Kerry was telling me stories about her partner's sister and husband who travelled with children, it sounded exciting and freeing. I thought, that's not me though, I couldn't do that. I don't think Adam would be bothered. I always wanted to go to Australia, Adam and I watched *Wanted Down Under*. I started to think whether that was something we could do. I asked Adam if he would move, and Adam said yes. I started to research it and try to find ways of how we could go.

I knew I didn't want to commit to Australia, I wanted to live there for a couple of years to experience it, so the only way was to get a sponsor. Adam was a builder and Australia wanted builders. I didn't want to give up our house either, so the only way that I figured we could do it was to take some money out so we had enough to support ourselves till Adam got a job, and to rent our house out for the time that we were there. I was excited, it felt like our dream was possible. I started to organise everything, gathered all the paperwork together, applied for a remortgage and researched to rent our house out. I thought it would be less stressful to rent our house out before we went, so that we were still here for a while if there were any teething problems and not having to rely on others to sort it for us. That meant we would need to move somewhere for a few months until we flew to Australia. Adam's Mum said we could move there.

I organised Paris and Jessica's medical reports and researched what would happen in regards to their hearts if we were over there. Researched the area and booked accommodation for two months to give us time to sort everything that we needed too while we were there, working out all the finances of our stay. I spoke to my work to see if they would give me leave for a year so that I could come back if I wanted to, and they said yes. I spoke to Paris's school and asked for work to take with us. Adam was self-employed so it was just finishing off jobs at his end and letting subcontractors know, which Adam sorted out, and he worked really hard on jobs to get more money in. I asked Adam if he minded my Mum coming with us for a month to experience Australia, then she could fly back home. Adam said yes and Mum said she wanted to; we all were really excited. All family and friends were great, really supportive, and obviously upset that we were leaving. We eventually moved in with Adam's Mum, which was really hard as Adam became really sick, which meant more pressure of outstanding jobs that needed completing before we went. This meant that I needed to continue to complete everything by myself, and travel to take the children to nursery and school, Adam eventually recovered and finished all his jobs.

Before taking off to Australia, my work had a training event that I was told I still needed to attend even though I was leaving. I can't remember where it was but we were to stay over. After the training we all settled to have a few drinks and a meal, I remember feeling really good, excited that I was leaving to go to Australia and I was telling everyone about it. The trainer was there and he seemed really interested in what I was saying, everyone was saying how lucky I was. I felt really happy and merry, and thought about Adam and the children, that we were soon to start a new journey together. I was chatting to everyone and I remember some lads came in and they bought me a few drinks. I woke up the next morning with my jeans and pants down my legs, laid on a board room table. I was in shock, what had happened? I felt woozy and still drunk. I can remember saying to myself, "No, this isn't happening," but it was, I was here in a board room with no idea how I got here and what had happened. I tried to reflect. I started to remember being outside having a fag, chatting to the trainer guy, then my next next memory I was on the floor trying to pull my jeans up. The trainer guy was laughing and kicking me, saying something, but I couldn't remember what. My manager was there and that is it, what had happened? I have known my manager for years, he wouldn't let that happen. I managed to walk back to my room, when I got there I started to cry, where was I? Was it real? What had happened? How could I have let this happen? It's my fault I shouldn't have got so drunk, but why couldn't I remember?

I checked my body. On my back there was what looked like a belt mark, how am I going to explain this to people, what are they going to think of me? I couldn't believe this was happening, what is wrong with me? I started to cry harder, a girl colleague came and knocked on my door, it was morning and it was time to go for breakfast. I was crying saying what I'd thought had happened from what I could remember. She looked shocked. I asked if she could remember seeing me, but she said I was drunk but that she had gone off to bed early. I said, "What am I going to do?" I couldn't stop crying. I explained the story to her and my intuition was telling me something had happened, that I might have been drugged. My other thoughts were don't be stupid, why would anyone do that? I have got drunk and done something stupid and now I am wanting to blame it on something else.

I was in distress. I needed to know what had happened, even if it was the fact that I was just drunk and had done something, I needed to know. I went down to breakfast and as soon as I saw some of the older guys, who I trusted from my team, I broke down crying. I told them my story, they said I needed to speak to my manager. I was frightened; what if it was just all in my head? What if I was wrong and was going to get someone into trouble? I was searching for answers, but everyone said they hadn't seen me with anyone and just that I was just drunk. Why would I be in the boardroom with my pants down and why would I have a belt mark on my back? I cried some more. My manager came over, I told him what I could remember and said I wasn't sure if I just dreamt it or not but it felt real. He looked shocked, he said he wasn't outside and didn't see me. I said that the hotel must have CCTV. I wondered if they would let me see it. The manager said they didn't have CCTV. I said I wanted to call the police. They all told me that I was just drunk, my manager said he would ring the trainer, which he did.

My manager said that the trainer wanted to speak with me when we got to head office. I was frightened but wanted to know the truth, so I agreed to meet him. I calmed down and we set off. I still felt really drunk. I met this guy in a room on his own and he said all we were doing was chatting, that I was drunk but nothing happened between us. I felt stupid but a part of me didn't believe him, part of me was saying why would he be so calm, had I made it all up, but it didn't explain why I was in that room with my pants down my ankles and a belt mark on my back. I started to feel disgusted with myself. I promised myself that I would never tell anyone. I am a mother and have a loving partner and I wasn't prepared to risk all that I had and was going to experience by being drunk, and not knowing the truth to what happened. I said I was sorry to the trainer, he said it didn't matter and reassured me that we have all been there. My manager let me sleep through the training. I kept having to go to the toilet to be sick and couldn't even drive home at the end of the day as I was still ill. Part of me kept saying that I have been drunk many times before and bits of the night always come back to me, so why wasn't this? That I stick to the same drink and don't drink anything else so I know how to handle Bacardi. I was dreading what might come back, but nothing did. I was that ashamed I couldn't tell Adam, I was fearful that it would destroy our plans, our future. I was frightened that he would see my back. I managed to hide the mark until it faded which seemed to take forever. When I got home I just hugged and kissed Adam and my children, telling them how much I loved them.

I was leaving work so I wouldn't have to face whatever people were saying about me, but the selective memories of that night were haunting me. I decided that I needed to tell someone so I told my Mum, and she agreed with me that something must have happened. I talked it through with her and decided that I was never going to find out and that if these guys did take advantage then they would have to live the rest of their lives with whatever happened. I obviously got myself checked over sexually, which all came back clear. A few weeks later Mum and Dad paid for a surprise leaving party and we were off.

Chapter 12

A New Beginning

Australia was amazing. Being in the sun and away from everyday life was freeing, I was excited and nervous. What if Adam didn't get a sponsor, were my thoughts, but then I would answer myself with, then we would have still had an amazing experience. We weren't long there when we heard that Australia had stopped the sponsoring because of the recession. Adam was gutted. I told him that there would still be a way, and that if he got himself out there to do a day of free work, people would connect to him and they would want him to stay. I moved to phone companies, asked Adam to phone, but he wouldn't move. I felt frustrated with him, why was he giving up just because of what we have heard? Adam wondered if I would be able to get a job instead, I felt angry. Does he not see all that I have done? I didn't have job skills that Australia was looking for, couldn't he just take responsibility just this once? Pressure was getting to us both; sexually I didn't want him to touch me, I felt it was always just about sex, no loving, no romance, no build up, plus I still also felt ashamed of what might have happened at the training event.

Mum looked after the kids so we could chat about our future. I needed to explain to him how I felt. I expressed that I couldn't see us staying together if things between us didn't change. If we didn't listen to each other and communicate how we felt, I felt I couldn't continue with our relationship. Adam voiced some of what he was unhappy about and we looked at our options, to try to stay or enjoy the time we had in Australia and go home afterwards. We decided we would enjoy our time and plan to go home, I felt better that we had a plan and communicated where we both were. I started to reflect on where I was in my life; I dreaded the thought of having to go home explaining to people that it had not worked out and back to the same routine, the same hamster wheel. I decided I would use the time in Australia to research studying counselling and our financial situation.

I did and there was financial support for mature students, I started to feel excited, I told Adam, I explained that what we would lose is just my car, the free petrol, and my bonus. That it would mean he would have to commit to bringing in a certain amount of money in each month, but that we could downsize our house to take the pressure off and build upon something run-down so that we would make money in the long run. Then once I was qualified we could look again at moving to Australia, and I would also have a skill that Australia wanted. Adam was unsure, but said if it was something that I really wanted to do that he would support me. I was so excited, so in love, he sees me. I started to plan and gather all the paperwork about Australia, contact everyone who we needed to organise work and things back home and we started to relax and enjoy our time.

We had met a couple who were from England. Their story of moving to Australia was brilliant: they had no money and had to live with friends, now they owned four houses and a boat. Adam was invited to go fishing with the guy. The night before I was on the phone to my Mum, as she had gone back home at this time, when Adam shouted me. I walked in to blood everywhere, Adam in shock and our Paris in his arms, blood was coming out of her eye. I went numb. I was aware of my panic but moved past it and grabbed a towel putting pressure on her eye, reassuring her that she was going to be OK. Adam had started to panic, saying he didn't mean to and had tears in his eyes. I looked at him and told him in a stern voice to pull himself together, that he better not to cry because he would panic our Paris. Our Jessica was stood there looking at the blood and saying, "Mum, look." I said calmly, "I know, it's blood, it's OK." We rushed straight to the hospital, and while sat in the car I remember looking at our Paris's eye and seeing a hole at the top of her eye socket. Fear washed over me. I felt like crying, but another part of me said not yet.

The hospital were brilliant. Adam was in distress and telling them the story. Paris had said, "Daddy, there is a fly." Flies in Australia were terrible at clinging to you. Adam hated them and was always killing them, stating that they were dirty. Adam had moved to pick up a wooden place mat and told Paris to sit down, he quickly swung the place mat to kill the fly, but Paris had stood up and he hit her right with the corner of the place mat. Adam was heartbroken. The hospital reassured him that she would be OK and that the experience will have affected him more than her. I was angry, though. Why does he always have to mess up? I held it in and didn't say anything as another part of me was saying it was an accident, leave him alone. I was in shock, thoughts running through my head. We got seen and they glued our Paris's eyelid. What if the impact had busted a bone and it affected her brain? What if he had hit her a little more to the left, and she would have lost her eye? Why can't he think before doing something?

We got home and my thoughts were still coming, I was really upset, Adam had fallen asleep snoring; I was laid there crying. He doesn't care. Where is my support? What about me? I was so angry with him. The next day I hadn't had much sleep and Adam was up ready to go fishing. I was shocked and commented, "What, you are still going?" Adam said sheepishly yes, that Paris was OK so he thought why not. I was hurt and angry but I held it in. I said what about me? Adam said, well, you are going out with his wife and kids. He didn't understand what I was meaning. I felt more hurt. I said angrily that I wasn't, and that I hadn't got much sleep last night thinking about everything that had happened, and that I was still worried about Paris and I didn't think he should go. Adam looked disappointed. I think he said, well, I will ring him then and tell him that I am not going. I felt for him. He had been looking forward to this for ages. I'd be OK if he goes, he had been so excited, were my thoughts, and now I was taking that away from him. I said that I would be OK and for him to go and to enjoy himself; once he had gone I felt so alone, so angry and so upset. Adam came back really excited about his day, which made me angrier; well, it's my own fault, I told him to go, were my thoughts. I tried to hide my anger but I am sure it came out in my responses to him.

It wasn't long before we eventually flew back home, we moved back in with Adam's Mum as our house was still rented out on a six month lease. I was OK about being back as I was excited at starting my new journey of study. I went back to work until August and let everyone know my plans for going to study counselling. Adam went back to work and started to build up more business. It was hard work again, managing everything and sorting everything out to get back into our house. I went to check on our house as I thought I was worried, as I had previously had a dream that the people who had been renting off us had done some structural changes. When I went in, I was shocked: it was filthy, our settee had pen marks all over it and it stank. I was upset but held it in, and thought it is just muck, I can sort it once we are back in.

The day came to get our house back. I was excited to have back our own space, the kids to have their playroom back. I went in to see a complete mess. The house was filthy – that filthy that you couldn't see through the shower and the toilets were black, there were stains on the carpets all upstairs, and in the garage was rubbish thrown all over. I was heartbroken, why would anyone do this? The people were due to come and give our keys back. I rang my friend Sue who lived on the same estate, nearly crying. Sue was shocked and really upset for me. I commented to Sue that I didn't think they would come and face me. With that a car pulled up, they both got out, I was fuming but I knew I needed to be calm. I kept telling myself, they live differently to me, their way of life is different. They walked in smiling, asking if I was glad that I was back, I looked at them thinking surely they are not real, they must know it is a disgrace.

I calmly said that I was upset at the state of the house. The woman said she tried to get a cleaner but she couldn't get one. I said you need more than a cleaner for this, that the muck was deeper than hiring a cleaner. The woman seemed shocked; she said it was not that bad. I pointed out that I couldn't see through the shower, that the toilets were black, that all the cupboards had greasy food all over them, that my carpets were ruined upstairs, that the garage looked like a dumping site. I asked her what was the house was like when I handed it over to her, she said it was lovely and I said, "And have you handed me back the same as what I handed to you?" This woman looked at me and went quiet. Her husband said, "When will we get the deposit back?" I looked at him and said there would be no deposit and that he would probably be getting a bill for the replacement of carpet and repainting to get the smell out of the house. The woman did seem to be sorry. I asked them to leave and said that I would sort it, I was so angry I was worried that I might say something that I would regret. They left and I just stood there and looked around. I said to Sue that I thought they would be OK as they were both doctors, as I started to cry.

Sue was amazing. She let us stay at her house while we cleaned, redecorated and got new carpets for our house. It was time to move in. It was lovely to be back. The tenant rang again to ask for his deposit back; I told him no chance and that I wanted £1,500 off him for everything else that I needed to replace and sort out. He said that he wanted to come and see me, as he didn't think it was as bad as I was making out. I agreed to see him. I was thinking that they do live differently to me and I wanted him to try to see my point of view, the difference of the house when I handed it over to when he handed it back. The guy came and accused me of making his wife ill, stating that because I had said the house was filthy she had become depressed. My first thoughts were what have I done, then my intuition was telling me I had be reasonable, that this guy's wife had recently had a baby and that was why she was depressed. I told him that I disagreed with him and wondered if he had considered that his wife might be suffering with postnatal depression. He seemed shocked then angry and said he wasn't prepared to pay any more money. I was angry and said, well, I will have to see you in court then, as I have pictures of the state of the house that you have left it in. With that he left. I was really angry with myself, something was telling me at that point of getting the house back to take photos. Another part of me said no, they wouldn't do that, they know that they have left it in a mess, so I didn't take any and just focused on getting it all sorted. I decided in the end that if I got some money back then great, if not then I would put it down to experience. We never did get any extra money from them.

We settled back into a routine, working, kids and spending time with family and friends. I had sorted all that I had needed to with college and researched that I would then go to university for three years to do a degree. It was the end of August and I had just finished with work. It was sad to say goodbye to everyone; I had been with the company for nearly ten years, I had learnt so much from them and I had worked hard too. I felt free to get away from the controlling structures that I felt had developed within this company, more rules and regulations had been applied that made it feel like I wasn't just doing my job, I was also gathering evidence to back myself up to show that I was doing my job, I felt that there was no trust and we all had become fearful that the managers were out to catch us out.

Reflecting back to when I first started, I felt it was fun and free working for them, you had targets to achieve but you were free to develop your own time management; that there were structures but bouncy structures, if you moved from them and achieved your targets it was OK. If you didn't achieve your targets there would be support to understand why and training to help you analyse your area more, managers left us alone and would be there to support and guide us whenever we needed them. Our team were all supportive of each other, ringing each other to encourage and guide one another, we had big areas as well and big targets, and we worked hard and played hard. When I left, there was always some report that needed completing to show where you had been or what you were doing, the areas were smaller and so were the targets but it seemed harder to achieve. I believe on reflection now it was because I was fearful of getting things wrong, fearful of getting the sack because I had not hit target, my time was taken from visiting customers and enjoying the job to having to fill in forms in order to be trusted. The management and the company didn't seem to want to know, they had stopped listening to us and started to dictate; it had changed from the focus being on customers and staff to structures and profit. Our team was stressed and no one had any real time for each other. If you did give your time to a struggling colleague you wouldn't get seen by the management or the company and it would impact on your time trying to achieve targets. I was always an achiever, just never an over achiever because my time was used by management to train others, but that didn't stop them asking me why I was only a bit above target or why I had not seen a customer, or got the numbers on new business. It became tiring and time consuming having to keep explaining myself in order to be seen. I felt it had become a lonely job where everyone looked after themselves and didn't trust anyone else.

Chapter 13

Betrayal and Forgiveness

A few days before leaving I came home to Adam home early. I walked in and asked him how come he was back early? Adam started to cry. I asked what was wrong, he said he was unsure and needed space. I was shocked and confused; what was going off, why didn't I pick up that there was something wrong? Adam eventually said he was worried about me leaving work and the pressure being on him. Inside I felt angry; what about all the years I had the pressure? I held it in and said that if it didn't work out financially then I would have to go back to work, but that we wouldn't know until we tried. Adam said he was unsure about our relationship. My heart sank, was this really happening? Was he prepared to give everything up because he was scared? Adam said he wanted to go to his brother's for some time away to think. I was in shock and said OK.

Adam left and I broke down and started to cry. Maybe I am putting too much pressure on him? Maybe I shouldn't go to study? I phoned my Mum and Ella, they duplicated my thoughts. Do you think it's a good idea, Sharon? When I heard those thoughts back, anger would rise inside of me. Yes I do, it's about time he took some responsibility. This is what my dream is, I have supported him in building his business and going to Australia, I have worked hard to get here and it's not like I wouldn't still be sorting all the finances out and all that I originally do, all I am asking Adam for is to commit to bringing in a certain amount of money, which he usually brings in, it's just that he now needs to bring it in. The more I voiced where I was and what I was thinking the more angry I got. I also felt alone and disappointed, I felt that no one was on my side; maybe I was wrong? Is going to study worth losing my relationship over? What about our children?

I was also angry that Adam had taken off. With no communication I was lost, didn't know where I was, what was going to happen. I rang Adam, who seemed distant with me. I tried to stay calm and ask him to come home so we could talk, he said he needed time. I asked how much time. He said he didn't know. I was in pieces. How could he do this, why wouldn't he tell me what he was thinking? Ella saw that I was in distress and said that she would ring him, they were close so hopefully he would speak to her. Ella told me that Adam was angry on the phone and said that I was controlling, that he was fed up of me and that he wasn't prepared for me to go to study. I was distraught. I had only tried to do my best, I had given everything that I had. Our Ella suggested that maybe it was best that I didn't go and study. Anger built, and I said he can fuck off, I will do this with him or without him. I looked at our children, thoughts of 'they will go through what you did as a child' entered my head. Paris was only six, and Jessica three. I started to make a plan in my head of supporting myself and our children by selling the house and using the money to follow my dream.

After a few days Adam came to talk to me. He commented about me going to study, I said well, maybe I shouldn't then. Adam said, but it's your dream. I said I know, but if it means losing what we have and splitting up our family, is it worth it? Adam opened up some more and I started to get that old feeling in my stomach. Something wasn't right, there is more to this. I asked if there was anyone else. Adam told me not to be stupid. Adam had visited my Mum a few days before, crying, telling her how he felt. Mum had said that he needed to be careful what he was saying to me, as he was knocking nails into his own coffin. I confided in Mum that I felt that there was more to what Adam was saying and maybe there was someone else involved. Mum had told me that she thought Adam was having a nervous breakdown, I wondered whether she was right. This feeling told me it was more than that.

I started to search. A few weeks earlier Adam had got a job working for a guy who had lots of money. Adam would come home and tell me excitedly that this guy has a helicopter and that he said he can give him lots of work, that Adam used to go to school with his daughter. I remembered saying to Adam, laughing, don't you be taking off with a billionaire's daughter. I didn't think much more of it, but I had a dream that Adam was having an affair with her and I was crying to her Dad saying they had split up a family. The day after I just thought that I must have felt insecure about what he was telling me. Now these memories were coming back. I searched his phone bill, my heart pounding. On there were lots of messages to one number that he had been contacting for a few weeks, messages and phone calls early in the morning and late at night. I phoned our Ella and I explained everything. She asked what I was going to do. I said I was going to call the number and pretend I was the phone company asking if this was who I thought it was. That is what I did, and it was true – it was this guy's daughter's number.

I was numb. I sat on my own looking around our home, and photos of us as a family. I remembered him saying to our Ella that I was controlling, that's why he wasn't happy and was unsure about our relationship. Anger was building. Why had I been so stupid? Why did I not listen to myself? Why had he done this? Was I that bad? I must be, all the other guys cheated on me, it has to be me. Am I going to stay with someone who cheats and lies? There was no way, I would rather be on my own. I phoned my Mum and calmly told her all about it and asked if she would have our children that night so I could confront Adam and get him to leave. Mum was shocked. I remember her saying, "And I thought he was having a nervous breakdown." She asked if I was OK and seemed worried about what I might do. I reassured Mum that I wouldn't do anything, I just wanted Adam to be honest with me and needed our children away so that they didn't pick up on what's happening. Mum agreed to pick our children up, I phoned Adam and said that Mum was going to have Paris and Jessica that night to give us time to talk. Adam asked if I had sorted out his van insurance, I replied yes, but I hadn't. I went upstairs and packed Adam's clothes in bin liners and waited for him to come home. In this time I was reflecting on all that we had created and telling myself that I would be OK, that our children would be OK, that there was no way I will stay with a man I can't trust.

Adam came home and I asked him to sit down, he looked nervous and asked me what was going off. I calmly told him that I knew he had been having an affair, he said that I was stupid. I told him I knew who it was and explained that I had evidence of his phone bill. Adam started to laugh nervously and said it was just sex texting. I explained that I didn't care what it was, it was still cheating. I didn't get much more out of him and I started to feel upset, why wouldn't he now be honest? I just wanted him to go so I told him his bags were packed and that he could go to his Mum's. Adam seemed shocked and asked if I was joking. I said I wasn't and that as far as I was concerned, it was over. Adam took his things and got into his van, saying that I would regret it. I replied with, "I don't think so, and by the way your van has no insurance, sort it out yourself." Adam left and I went to get my phone. I phoned the number he had been texting and calmly explained who I was, that I know about their affair and that Adam was now single so she could have him. I also said that I hoped that she could sleep at night knowing that she had split up a family of four and that I am sure her Dad will be so proud of his daughter when I called to tell him, all I heard back from her was 'we were just texting'. I put the phone down, and I broke down and cried. Not long after Adam rang me, I dried my tears and composed myself and answered. He wanted to know what I had said to this girl, as she had phoned him distraught. I replied, angry, that she was very lucky that I hadn't gone up to where she works and created a scene, that I wasn't interested with how upset she was. With that I put the phone down and cried some more.

Family and friends were shocked and really supportive. I didn't hear anything from Adam's family, which really upset me. Adam had tried to say sorry and had been around, upset, saying he had made a mistake. I told him he shouldn't be saying sorry to me, that he should say sorry to our two daughters. I wasn't interested in listening to him. I was closed, hurt, angry and sad. I told him that I was putting the house up for sale and that he could have whatever was left, after I took my money back from what I had shared from the home I owned on my own when we had met. Adam wasn't happy about this but I told him it was tough shit, when you play with fire you can get burnt. Adam had phoned our Ella crying, saying how sorry he was. He explained that he had been so disappointed that things had not worked out in Australia that he was coming back to his old life, his shit van with no money, and then this girl has started to flirt with him. Adam was surprised and flattered that she seemed interested and it had started off as a bit of fun, that nothing had happened other than texting, but now he saw that it was like he had been cheating. Our Ella asked if I would take him back, I said no.

A week or so later I was out in town when I saw Adam's brother Dan, he said, "Hey up Shaz," as if nothing had happened. I was shocked. How can you be OK? were my thoughts. I started to cry. "Why have you not phoned me to check whether me and the kids are OK?" I asked. "I can't believe that you think it is OK what your brother has done." I said a few other things and Dan said, "Maybe you need to look at yourself." I was distraught. I went home and phoned Adam, crying down the phone, asking him why, asking him to look at what he has done. Adam became upset too and said he was sorry. I calmed down and we talked some more. Adam asked if he could come and talk. I said I was unsure. It was middle of September, I had started college and it was nearly my birthday. Our Ella suggested that Adam come on my birthday to their house so that we could talk. I agreed.

Adam asked again if we could try again. I remember my Dad's words ringing in my ear of what he had said to me a few weeks earlier. "Sharon, look at me and your Mum, sometimes it is worth it to try again." Could I ever trust him again? How would we get through this? What about our children? What would it be like for them? What about what happened before I went to Australia? Am I just as bad, and I haven't told Adam? Maybe this is my comeuppance? What goes around comes around. Other thoughts were, but I was drunk or drugged, I didn't mean to do whatever I did or didn't do. There would be no way I would do that being sober, to risk losing my family, or to hurt Adam like that. A strong thought was, did I want to be the one that decided that we wouldn't be a family any more? I was in internal conflict and really confused, upset and fearful.

I decided that we could see how things go but I couldn't make any promises. It was hard, building that trust back up, and only a few months later Adam had gone out and I had that feeling in my stomach again. I again put it down to feeling insecure. I said to Adam that he had better be back at a reasonable time, he said he would. I couldn't sleep properly. Five am came and I heard a door of a cab; I was still half asleep and couldn't see what taxi it was. Adam had just got in. I was fuming. He jumped into bed completely drunk. I checked his phone, there was a number on there at three am. I rang it and a man answered. I put the phone down. I knew this was going to happen, I was telling myself. Why did I let him go out, were my thoughts, other thoughts were don't be stupid, I can't stop him from going out, do I really want to be with a man that I have to watch and keep an eye on?

Where had he been? Who had he been with? What am I doing taking him back? I can't believe he is prepared to risk it all again. I woke him up. "Where you been?" I couldn't get anything out of him so I left it till he woke, firing all questions at him, he couldn't remember, where he went, who he was with. I didn't believe him. I told him that I would not sleep with him until he got sexually tested and if he refused we were over. Adam did and he was clear but I still had that gut feeling. I told myself I could either keep distrusting him and searching or let this go and promise myself from now on I will listen to myself next time and move on. I let it go. There were other times that I felt insecure, but didn't have that gut feeling as before so I would tell Adam and he would reassure me that he loved me and that I had nothing to worry about as he would never cheat again. It took a good couple of years to build back trust and if I am honest, there wasn't complete trust. I didn't fully trust him with money, I didn't fully trust him to tell me the complete truth, but I accepted that and just thought I would listen to my gut if anything else was to happen, so this helped me to relax my thinking and we were a family, building a future together... but deep down something was telling me it would happen again. I chose to ignore it.

Chapter 14

Building Self-awareness

Our Jessica and Paris were growing so fast, Jessica was three and Paris six. I had taken our Jessica to all her heart appointments and she still had a low heart rate. I got a phone call from the hospital, they told me that they had a meeting about our Jessica and what they were going to do about her low heart rate. The doctor told me that the holes wouldn't close up on their own and that they had decided that she would need an operation, but that they were hoping to do keyhole surgery. Jessica would have to come back in for more tests to see if that was the way they could operate. I was upset but thought, well, at least she wouldn't have to go through what our Paris did. I took Jessica in and a few days later the doctor rang to say that she was sorry but it would have to be open heart surgery. I was devastated. I started to cry. After a while a part of me said that she would be OK, that we would be OK, we have been through it before and we know what to expect. That it would be different this time as Jessica was older, stronger and could tell us if she was in pain. I started to feel better. The doctor had explained that it would be probably happen next year when Jessica was four, which is when I would be in my second year of university. I phoned everyone to let them know. Adam was really worried but I reassured him that we would be OK, our Jessica would be OK.

I finished college and got into Leeds University, on the course that I wanted. It was a course that I thought would suit me, applying theory in a practical way and personal development. I was frightened, though – what if it didn't work out? What if I was just not clever enough? I always believed that I wasn't academically clever.

I never did well at school so what would make me think I could go to university? Another part of myself would say that I had learnt in employment and completed courses, so it is just applying myself in another way, plus I was older now and this was something I was really interested in. When I started university I remember feeling as if I was home; it felt right, even though my fear was still there. I acknowledged that I was fearful of failing. I would tell myself that I could always go back to do what I used to do, that to fail is not to try. These thoughts made me strong enough to keep turning up at university. I remember one of the tutors, Roger, telling us 'this course will change you'; I remember feeling fearful and thinking no one was going to change me.

I had met a lady who was similar age to me. I was 32 years old. Her name was Heidi; we clicked and got on easily. All the other students were 18 to 25, which I didn't see as a problem as in my own thinking I always felt young. I settled into student life, but I always felt guilty for being there as if I should be working, as if I was lazy because I wasn't grafting. This feeling took three years to leave me. It didn't help that other people would wind me up taking the piss, saying I had it easy being a student. I thought that they didn't have a clue. I would try to defend myself, but felt never seen, so I stopped trying and stopped listening to them. Whilst at university I realised that even though I was doing a degree I would still have to complete another two years of a diploma to get a practitioner certificate. I was gutted; how did I miss that, what would Adam say? Well, I would have to work as well if we needed the money, as the last two years were part time. I told Adam he wasn't pleased but I reassured him that I would work as well. I told myself that it would give me more time to take everything in, to learn at a deeper level, that this would benefit me.

I was wary of the tutors on the course to start with. They all seemed nice but I felt frightened that they could see me and all that I am. The theory I loved, but felt frustrated with; there was so much and it all conflicted with the other and the language was so complicated.

I remember being in theory and not getting what Ben, the course leader, was saying. I voiced what I thought he was saying into what I call normal language but what I mean is common language. Ben agreed that what I was saying was the same as what the theory meant. I felt angry again; I asked, why have they used big words? Is that to make it more expensive? Ben just smiled at me and shrugged his shoulders as if to say 'I don't know'. I was so angry, why can't people just be honest and use simple language? Then we would all understand so easily and everyone could benefit from understanding how and why we develop the way we do.

We learnt all the theory in psychotherapy. I loved learning all the different theories and loved debating about them. I started to see theory within my own life experiences. I would take on theory that sat with me and my life experiences, and the parts that didn't I would hold and wonder why? Where does this fit? Part of myself would say it was wrong, or not meant in that way. It was frustrating as it caused me to be in internal conflict, I used to come home with a headache. I would always be eager to go back the next day and learn more, though. I loved university, I loved learning, I loved the personal development sessions learning about myself, building safe attachments where I felt safe enough to explore my feelings and thoughts. It became apparent that I struggled to show my feelings. I would use words but they were constructed sentences not feelings, even though I would feel my feelings and other people's inside, they didn't seem to come out when I tried to express myself. I remember Paul, one of the tutors in counselling sessions, saying to me that I just needed to retune myself rather than always moving cognitively to save people, that I was doing all the work for them. I was frustrated and would tell him that I didn't know what he meant, then we would both look at each other and laugh. I knew I was learning, but I was frustrated with myself at the time it was taking me to understand, comparing myself negatively with others who seemed natural at it all. Part of myself was telling me I wasn't relaxing, therefore I wasn't truly listening, but I couldn't control my mind from wanting to solve. I wanted to analyse and find the answers, so that people would be safe. No, end of times, I thought, this is too hard, I am never going to be any good, but my heart would always skip a beat at new information, new insight that I would get from my own life experiences that would encourage me and give me the strength to carry on.

After my first year at university we received our Jessica's date for her operation it would be in October 2011. I would have only been back at university for a month, in my second year. I was worried for Jessica and the time I would need off uni. I told the tutors what was happening and they told me to take the time that I needed and to find someone who would gather class notes for me.

The day of our Jessica's operation arrived. I was nervous but nothing like what I was like with Paris. Jessica was brilliant, she took it all in her stride, getting ready for surgery. I think Adam and my Mum went in with Jessica for her to be put under; I didn't feel like I could do it. Adam came out crying and Mum was supporting him, we wandered around waiting for the phone call to say that she was out of her operation. I think it was about four hours, the same as our Paris, when the hospital rang to say Jessica was in recovery. Through that time I was in my own little world, having limited interaction with my Mum and Adam. It helped me cope, I felt safe there, I was telling myself she would be OK, that she would recover quickly and we would all soon be back to living our lives.

We rushed up to see our little girl crying, telling us that she was thirsty. I asked if she was allowed anything to drink, she was allowed to suck on a sponge which was dipped into water. It wasn't enough and Jessica told us she was still thirsty, they eventually gave her an ice lolly. Jessica was soon on the ward and was her happy carefree self; she didn't moan once. The next day she was out of bed walking around the ward, it was astonishing to see. A few days later the nurses said that if it wasn't the weekend, Jessica could have gone home with how she was recovering. I was shocked; really, would they have let her go? Monday arrived and they were preparing for us to leave. Jessica needed to have a few stitches out which she was fearful of and started to cry. I told her that this was nothing compared to what she had been through and for her to think of how brave she had been. Eventually she let the doctor do what he needed to do and we were walking out of the hospital when she fell over. My heart was in my mouth. She quickly stood up and said, "I am OK," and smiled. I couldn't believe her, my brave little girl.

Jessica had no problem healing and getting on doing all the things she wanted to do. I would be worried and she would tell me she was fine, so I allowed her to do what she felt she could. On return visits to the hospital they told us Jessica still had a low heart rate and they would just monitor her, as it could just be her way, or change as she gets older. They said she might have to have a pacemaker when she is older but nothing would be decided until they have had time to monitor her and she has had time to grow. It was disappointing but I figured that we would deal with that when and if it comes, and we all got back to our lives and routines.

We had put our house up for sale, but the house prices had started to fall. I knew we needed the asking price to be able to use the money to renovate another house so that we could live comfortably without sacrificing too much in space. We had offers that were £70,000 lower than our asking price, then offers that were £20,000 lower; it came to a point where two people were after our house £20,000 lower. I discussed it with Adam and Ella. Both of them were saying that I should consider them, as they believed that I wouldn't get what I wanted for it. Another part of me was telling me to wait. I rechecked my workings out, we would struggle and wouldn't have enough money to complete another house, but what if we lost these potential buyers? We couldn't continue to pay for the mortgage we had and needed to sell as soon as possible. Other thoughts were telling me that I would get the asking price for it, but in reality it wasn't looking like we would. After a while I phoned the estate agents back and begrudgingly said I would accept the first offer. The woman said she would get back to me, she did and told me the first people had moved to buy another house, so she would go to the second people. The woman couldn't get hold of them, so we waited; it turned out that they had changed their minds. I felt deflated. I should have accepted straight away, it served myself right for being too greedy, I told myself.

A few weeks later I was at university when I received a phone call from the estate agents, she said there was a woman who viewed our house a few months ago and wanted to put an offer on our house. I wasn't excited or bothered, I just thought here we go again, haggling to get the best price. I said snappily, "What are they offering?" The woman said, "The asking price." I was shocked and excited. "Really?" I asked. "Yes," said the estate woman, laughing. I said, "Well, how can I refuse such an offer?" with a smile on my face. I had thoughts of what if they backed out? Was I being too greedy? But another part of myself would say that our house was worth what I was asking. Everyone else was also shocked. We sold and moved in with Mum for a year to renovate the new house we had brought. It was hard work, Adam was working really hard through the day and then working on our house at nights and weekends. I was at university all day, organising and looking after our children on nights and weekends, managing our finances and completing my assignments, but I knew it would be all worth it in the end.

Adam and I would have disagreements about money and searching for the best price; my argument was we needed to be organised so our money would go further. Adam would order things and I would ask how much it had cost, he would get angry and say they wouldn't rob me. I would get so frustrated, and tell him we needed to know, and explain that how was I supposed to manage our money when I don't know how much stuff costs? Adam would say that he knew, I said well, tell me then. This would be a repeated argument that kept going round and round. We had lived at Mum's for over a year, and I would ask Adam when he thought we would be in by; the date kept changing which was so frustrating. I used to say to him, why don't you overestimate everything, that way people don't get disappointed when what you tell them is wrong? He wouldn't listen.

Adam had an opportunity to work away which was good money, but it meant that our house would be on hold. We managed to get other people into help out so that we could get in faster. We moved in July. There was still a lot to do, but I thought if we were in then it would be easier as we were there. It was hard work being in an unfinished house with two children, seeing all the things that needed to be completed, it felt that we never got a rest. Adam was going back to working away and it was nearly winter. I kept saying that we needed the heating sorting as it would be too cold for us. Adam had not managed to sort it and went and worked away. I was so angry but held it in; I could see that every other job would come first before us as a family, not making sure we were secure and safe. I expressed this to Adam on the phone with anger, he said that he was trying but the other jobs brought the money in, he moved to organise someone to do the heating. I told myself he was trying his best and I calmed down. I analysed where we were in every way: financially, time wise, and I identified we had no balance. I explained to Adam that I knew we needed the money but I could see that if he was more organised he would have more time. I tried to show him where he was losing time by not forward-thinking, such as having to go to B&Q four or five times a day. Adam would take offence. I would question myself about how I have approached him: did I do it in a loving way or with anger? On reflection I would say I communicated in both ways, but it didn't seem to matter which way I moved to show him or tell him, he always seemed to think that I was attacking him and he would comment that I thought I was perfect. I would wonder what the point was, he couldn't see that I was trying to help.

A few months later Adam came to me to say he had messed up on a job and that we needed £4,000 for him to complete the job. I was so upset, was he for real? We were living in a house that was not complete and we were running out of money to complete it and he wanted to use £4,000 of our money, that we hadn't got? I was so angry, I told him that I had enough, that he was not using any of our money and that I suggested that he needed to go back to his clients and be honest with them that he had made a mistake and needed more money. Adam said that he couldn't do that. I was getting angrier; he wouldn't go and ask for more money on a job that he had under-priced. These clients knew they were getting an extension really cheap, but he would risk his own family security, what, to not look bad? Adam had already worked on this job for about five weeks and only received £2,000 from it, so really we had lost more than £4,000 as he still had a few weeks left to work. I pointed this out to Adam but he didn't want to see it. I told Adam that if he chose not to go back to his clients to ask for more money then we would be over, that I couldn't do this any more. I really meant it, I had had enough. I didn't want to be with a guy that wouldn't consider his family first, that didn't want to learn from his mistakes and wouldn't be honest when he did mess up. Adam did go back and speak with his clients and ended up getting another £2,000 off them. I still wasn't happy but I thought, well, at least he did admit his mistake and got more money.

I was learning loads from university and I would come back and share my knowledge with Adam. Adam didn't seem interested and sometimes I would think it would be great to be with a guy who wants to have deeper conversations. Other thoughts would come and I would tell myself, Adam is a great guy, leave him alone. I would tell myself that I was never satisfied and that Adam always tried his best. I would move to share with my family and friends too, but again most of them didn't seem that interested, Ella would say don't you think you are too deep? My response, now being at university, would be no, on reflection I felt more empowered that I wasn't alone. People in university were like me, famous people even thought like me. My friends Jan and Ruth had greatly supported me through university, checking over my work, helping me to build my confidence. I was getting stronger and stronger, starting to believe in myself, that one day I would be a counsellor. I had finished my degree and I was really pleased with my results, it was hard work but I loved every moment of it.

It was time for me to start my diploma, and in another two years I would be qualified as a counsellor/psychotherapist; I could see my dream. The plan was to build my private business to give me flexible time to be with our children. Adam was building a garage with rooms at the top, at the bottom of our garden which I would use as my therapeutic house and on weekends we could use it for parties and people staying over. I could see that we would be in an amazing position where I was earning as well as Adam. I imagined Adam having more time to enjoy the things he loved like fishing, we would get excited together and he would say he was going to buy a kayak so he could fish on the river Don. We now had a low mortgage, low bills and a great house that still wasn't finished but it would be, and soon we would have more money to travel and do all the things we would love to do as a family. I would be doing a job that I loved, life would be easier and happier, and we would be more financially free.

I loved being back at university, with the same tutors. Heidi, my friend, had moved; it was sad to see her go but I knew we would always be friends. I was excited to meet new students but also nervous, there was a couple of us who were moving onto the diploma but others had decided to either study elsewhere, travel or find work. I quickly made friends with everyone but I was drawn to Debbie and Lee, who had known each other training on their certificate. I seemed to feel relaxed more than everyone else, and perceived it was because I already knew the tutors and the structure of Leeds University. I promised myself that I would share my knowledge with everyone in a hope that it would make it easier for them to settle. The diploma was more practical than the degree, which I was excited about, getting more involved in placements and supervision. We also had personal development as well as theory; I loved it all and perceived that the course had a good balance. I also knew that the tutors were amazing people, with knowledge as well as personal wisdom. I told myself that I would learn and take everything in from everyone and use this time effectively as I had decided not to work and figured that we would struggle through as I wanted to dedicate my commitment to all of it, and gain as much experience as I could from my placements. Adam wasn't happy, but I managed the finances and knew we could do it. It would mean that things would just still be tight for the next couple of years. I explained this to him and also tried to point out that we had not done too bad to say I had not been working for four years but that we still managed to go on holiday every year, and do most of what we wanted to do.

At university I was aware that I seemed to be the one who was always talking, always asking questions. I would sometimes crucify myself; other people are here to learn as well, stop taking all the space, I would tell myself. I would hold myself back to keep quiet and allow other people time to speak. They didn't seem to, so another part of myself would say speak up, don't waste this time to learn as much as you can. I voiced my fears in personal development, most people felt that I did speak more than anyone else but that they were fine with this and they liked what I questioned and how I gave my version of things. I felt more at ease and would question and speak up with ease, I would still give time to others but if I felt that they weren't going to use it, I would.

I remember one day being in theory and another peer pulling a face when I spoke and being really funny with me. I asked her if I had done anything wrong to her, this lady commented that it irritated her how I always had something to say. Part of myself was telling me that she was jealous, but another part of me was saying she was right and that I shouldn't speak up. The voice of my positive side had become stronger, though, and I responded that there was nothing stopping her from speaking up. I explained that I was there to learn and I would use the time wisely. This lady seemed to back down and commented how I was the leader of my group and she was the leader of her group. I was shocked; I didn't see myself that way, I didn't think I was better than any of the peers in my group. I appreciated them all and what they had to say, I learnt from everyone. I acknowledged that I spoke more and inputted more, but I didn't want to be more powerful than anyone. I was worried. Is that what everyone else thought? I voiced my concerns and what I had experienced within my personal development group, I wanted to know if they felt I was like that. Everyone was surprised and shocked at what this lady had said and reassured me that they didn't feel that I felt higher than them, or the leader of our group, and that none of them felt inferior to me. A few said they felt inspired by me, they wondered where this all sat within me, why was I worried about what she or anyone else thought. I didn't know, but I promised myself I was going to find out.

I started to look deeper at myself, wondering why and memories of being a child about nine or ten came back to me. I was the captain of our netball team, I had been nominated by my team mates. One day we were all supposed to meet, but none of my team were there, I went to look for them they were all in the school hall with our teacher. I said that I was sorry that I didn't realise that we all was meant to be meeting in here. Our teacher said, "It's OK, Sharon, now that you are here your teammates can tell you why they have called a meeting behind your back." I was confused and felt upset. Why didn't they tell me? What had I done wrong? This teacher explained that my teammates didn't want me to be captain of the netball team any more. I remember feeling upset and thinking, I don't want to be captain if my friends are going to fall out with me. I think I said that I didn't mind someone else being captain. Our teacher was having none of it. She asked everyone to tell me why they didn't want me to be captain any more. A few of my teammates stood up and told me in different ways why they didn't want me to be captain any more; what I heard was that I had been bragging about being captain. Afterwards our teacher said that they were all jealous and told us all that I was staying captain of our netball team as I was the best person for the job, that it was her decision, and that was the end of that. I felt uneasy with my teammates, I didn't want to be captain if it meant I would lose my friends. I told myself that I didn't ever want to make anyone jealous of me again, that I must have been bragging about being captain for them to become jealous. I realised that I had formulated a belief as a child that I made people jealous by telling them what I loved and how well I thought I was doing. As a child I had made a decision that I would always put others first before myself, as I believed as a child that by doing this I would never experience people being jealous of me or lose their love.

I felt empowered to know and understand why I was so worried about this lady perceiving me a certain way; I also felt excited and free to learn about myself. I loved personal development and I was eager to learn more and look deeper to give myself more understanding, more self-awareness. As a group we had developed an amazing relationship with each other, where we all moved to open up more and create honesty and openness between us. I acknowledged that our tutor was accepting and loving, always giving us time to understand ourselves and each other; we would laugh, we would cry, we would get angry, disappointed, frustrated all different emotions and all of us at some point would share them with each other, connected to different life experiences in our past or our present about other people outside of our group or connected to each other within our group. The course had taught us to try to own our emotions, to encourage us to always try to start off with 'I feel... this way because'. On reflection, it wouldn't happen that way to start with, and we would say, "You made me feel..." or, "They made me feel..." but whatever we said would be accepted and be gently challenged by our tutor. I acknowledged there were lots of times I would feel nervous about getting things wrong, but I would still push myself to speak up as I felt safe that if I did get it wrong I would be questioned but in a loving way. I wonder why you said that? What were you feeling and thinking at that time? This always helped me come back to me and feel safe to explore myself some more.

Chapter 15

Time to Understand and Heal

Every time I would get personal insight I would feel empowered; I had started my own personal counselling and I was excited and nervous about what I was going to unearth. University and my placements were going well, our children were settled in their new school and Adam had started to work away again, we were all busy with trying to finish the house off but I could see an ending and would comment to Adam that it wouldn't be long now.

I loved my experience of counselling and I was learning fast about my emotions and thoughts that I had hidden through fear of hurting the ones that I loved. My counsellor accepted me in anything I was saying; don't get me wrong, the first few times I was frightened, but just who she was, her presence, put me at ease. I loved that I had somewhere and someone safe to explore all that I felt stuck in or what I was still in pain with, connected to my past and/or present experiences. I acknowledged that once I had understanding I would go back to the people my experiences connected to, such as Mum, Dad, Adam, Ella, friends, in order to explain where I was or what I had felt, owning my emotions. I gained further insight into where they were, and through me opening up and being honest they seemed to, too. If they didn't most of the time, I was able to just accept that is where they are and let go, or if I couldn't I would bring it back up within my counselling session to look deeper at any other emotions, experiences and thoughts to seek why I couldn't let go. I had discussed my experiences of abuse with my counsellor and explained that after the first abuse I was OK, she seemed to believe me and get that I was OK. This was the first person that I felt heard me, saw me and accepted that I was OK. I always felt that when I ever said that before, people were thinking that I was lying, that there was no way that I could be OK with being abused, but not my counsellor, she believed me. I explained that I felt that I had got stuck within that experience because of other experiences and because I had nowhere safe to explore what had happened to me, that I had talked to my Mum a lot but held stuff back because I knew it was painful for her to remember.

I would use any spare time to reflect on my experiences of my abuse and remember that Keith and Barry were both kind in lots of ways, they both had taught me things. Keith gave me responsibility and trust. Barry had shown me how someone could change from being loving and fun through fear to becoming nasty and vindictive. Other thoughts would come, saying it's because they were manipulating, I am naive, but another part of myself was telling me that these memories were the goodness in them both, that both of my abusers were and could be also kind and loving men. I reflected on my movement of hurting men, teasing them, wanting to control them. I reflected on my experience with Barry when I told him that I would stab him, and that I was frightened of myself because I knew I could have done it. Through my analysis of my experiences I now knew that at that time I was in pain and in anger. That I had developed not to show my emotions to others so therefore I couldn't see myself; I was ignoring my emotions, that they would build to the point where I didn't have control, is this what had happened to them? I wondered what had happened to Keith. What had happened for him to behave in such a way? What had he experienced in his past? What had been his thoughts and emotions? I knew I had healed and I wasn't in pain any more because I understood myself within those experiences and the after effects of my behaviour. I had acceptance for myself within my experiences and when I reflected, I didn't feel pain or anger in the present moment. I could reconnect to that pain and anger but it would leave me as soon as I stopped reflecting.

I wanted to find out Keith's story but I was frightened. What if he reacts and does something? What if he starts to follow me? I have children, what about their safety? What would people think? What would my Mum say? Another part of myself, which at this point I could identify as my intuition, told me that he was the one who was scared and frightened, not me, that I had moved to heal, to understand, to accept and that I could keep creating fear with these thoughts but then it would stop me from knowing Keith's truth. I decided I would write him a letter and then make the decision whether to send it or not. I told Adam who said it was up to me, but I told no one else. After writing the letter I wondered to myself why I was sending it. Was it to get recognition for what he had done? It wasn't; my intuition was telling me to send it to gain understanding and I was telling myself that there would be understanding that might help others at a later point, to also understand and acknowledge why we all move in different ways and at different levels in hurting each other.

I moved to speak with my Mum before I sent the letter as I felt that I would be betraying her if I didn't, but I was adamant I was sending it though even if she said not to. Mum was shocked and a bit angry, but I showed her my letter which explained why I wanted to send it. Mum said that it was up to me but that she didn't want me to put my address for him to return any letters he writes. Mum suggested that I use her address, as he knows where she lives so it didn't matter, plus she wanted to read the letters. I agreed to what she wanted me to do and I sent it, I was nervous and soon I was to get a response.

I had explained in my letter to Keith why I was writing to him, that I felt more me to be able to write to him. That I had forgiven his behaviour towards me and that I was unsure of where he was at this moment in time, meaning whether he owned and accepted his behaviour towards me or whether he still felt he had done nothing wrong. I explained that I felt that it didn't really matter to me whether he had or not, and explored why I was writing to him. I told him that I wanted him to know that I now could see and admit the love that he showed me, the time he spent with me explaining things, teaching me how to cook and the trust that he gave me in managing the shop. I explained that to me love is a connection of acceptance and of equal control, and that when the abuse started the control had shifted and for me that wasn't love. That I understand he told me that I should have just told him to stop and that it would have, but we both knew it shouldn't have started.

I questioned and wondered to myself where he had learned this from, what was his life story? I told him I remembered feeling fearful and anxious going to his Mum's house and to see his brother at dinner time. That as a child I didn't and still don't understand why. That I was asking him to tell me why.

I explained that I would understand if he didn't want to look at this and I would accept his decision, but that I felt that through us all sharing our experiences of life truthfully we can all learn and develop to gain self-awareness and inner control, which I perceive gives us freedom to become who we want to become.

A week or so later Keith responded with:

> *I have just read your letter for the 50th time, I read between the lines as well. The letter you wrote to me and this one I am writing to you I think of as private just between you and me. I would be happy if you thought the same. Thank you for your forgiveness. There is an excuse for nothing and a reason for everything. So, I will not make an excuse for upsetting you and will take full responsibility, I cannot think of a good reason. I obviously have done something wrong or you would not have got upset. I am sorry.*

> *You sound very adult and in control in your letter. How do you find your Real Me? Is it through religion, medication or your own personality coming through? Please write again as you have really got me thinking.*

> *Yours*
> *Keith*

P.S. Sorry for taking so long to reply, as you can see I am not very good at writing. I am better at reading.

I felt frightened when I received Keith's letter. After speaking with my counsellor and my Mum, I acknowledged that my thoughts were, he is going to try to manipulate me and this interlinked with Keith asking for our letters to be private. I acknowledged this also interlinked with the experience of the abuse, of knowing what was happening but also developing thoughts that would question that knowing, questioning myself as the situation wasn't showing abuse was happening; Keith was talking to me as he moved to abuse me as if he wasn't doing anything wrong. I felt empowered knowing where I was and I decided to respond.

Thank you for your apology. Firstly, I want to be honest and make you aware that I cannot commit to keeping our contact private, I hope that within this letter I will be able to give you an insight into why I feel the need to share our contact.

I get the feeling from your letter that there is fear as to whom I will share the contents of that letter or future letters with. I want to make it clear that my decision to make contact with you is not for revenge.

I feel I have been very fortunate within my life, because I have experienced people who love me, who accept me and who are supporting of me being me even though they may not share or understand my feelings or thoughts, they still stand by ME. The real me is not influenced by religion or medication but by my own subjective experiences and how I have come to understand them which I feel is connected to my inner feelings, these are not feelings that are created through thought alone but are more gut feelings, a knowing if this makes sense.

I have experienced pain and encountered many people who are in pain. I have found personally that pain, fear, uncertainty can be healed through sharing. I shared my pain, fear and uncertainty with my Mum and what she did was so healing. Mum listened, didn't judge, didn't question me, she accepted me, my thoughts, feelings and behaviour. Through this and my counselling experience I have been able to forgive you and my other abusers.

I questioned many times who I would have become if I never had that loving attachment/connection, the unconditional love? Would have I become so absorbed in hatred and pain that I could have lost myself forever? Projecting that pain, fear, hatred onto others? Would I have been able to cope keeping it all to myself?

After the abuse came out I felt lost, lost because people didn't want to understand why. Their answers would be, it was evil. This didn't help me, I felt lost because I needed to understand why. My connection with you was more than just evil, there were so many different experiences that were also of love and support, unfortunately the abuse tarnished these memories for many years.

I feel that the more I accept and understand my life experiences (whether that be happiness or sadness) the more me I become. The less fear and uncertainty has hold of me, the more I have control, control of me, no one else, just me. The more self-awareness I develop of my process, why I reacted the way I did, my thoughts and feelings, the more control I have in deciding whether to change or not and in how I react to things and people. This process is echoed through psychotherapy and I find there are other people who have experienced similar healing in counselling.

I have been studying for the last five years and my dreams are to help people understand themselves through love, acceptance and genuineness of my connection with them. I feel blessed to be who I am and to have had the experiences I have had, but mainly to have had the love of people around me. I believe that if I hadn't felt the love you showed me then I would have not ever made a decision to contact you. I would have never questioned why, and further questioned, why do people perpetrate? Why do we all hurt each other in some way or another?

I feel having more understanding of your life experiences will help me in having empathy in other people's experiences. I feel I can learn a great deal from you but also know I am asking a lot, that means you have to trust me and the people I share these letters with. Again I will accept if you decide not to go there and thank you again for your apology.

Keith responded with:

Wow I've finally got the message, thank you. I have always been a bit slow, even before I had all the bangs on the head. (they were real, I did not make them up) I do not get fear or upset anymore, I am just WARY. I have done good things in my life (I am still doing some) as well as bad. That's why I do not want to get side-tracked or diverted. You can ask me anything you want and I won't get upset. I will not tell you any lies, I will tell you the truth or say I cannot answer at this time. Do not forget equal control, I am as interested in your life story as much as you are in mine. One of the main reasons I trusted you to run the shop was if you got it right you got it right, if you got it wrong you got it wrong, there was never any lies. I assume you have not changed? Your letters are much better than mine, why? I do not write letters anymore (like most people). What about you? That first letter you wrote me that I replied to was very thought provoking. How many other people have you written to? And how many replies have you had?

If you want my life story, it will be easier for me to start now and go backwards than for me to start at zero and go forwards. You go the way that is best for you. I have got a problem. Only one person reads your letters to me, that is ME. How many people will read my letters to you? 5 or 10 or 50? I do not have fear, I am just wary.

144

At the moment, I have got no wife, girlfriend living with me, just one dog and three cats so in theory I should have plenty of spare time but things do not always work out like that. I am running the shop on my own at the moment, all small shops are having problems at the moment but I make just enough to help other people a bit. I'll give you two small examples of how I have helped people. Three years ago I was invited to go to Africa to stay with local people (not living in a hotel). One day we were going to the market to buy some food, on the way to the market we passed an old lady on the street corner trying to sell some fruit, she looked as though she had been there forever. It takes a long time to shop in the market in Africa but on the way back she was still there so I asked the girl from the family who was with me to ask how long she had been there, she said all day. She had not eaten all day or the day before either and if she could not sell some of her fruit or beg, borrow or steal fifty pence, yes 50p not £50, she would not eat, the next day as well (only her own fruit). I bought all of it so at least she could eat for two or three days. The first thing I bought in Africa was a bike, it's walk or bike in that area there is nothing else. If you have a bike you are a somebody. The locals move everything on bikes. There are no vans, cars or roads. The problem is that they cost a lot of money (about £80, or three months' wages if you have a job, which nobody has). There is no state money there, no social security, no family allowance, child benefit or old age pension, NOTHING. People were coming from miles around to see the white man living in the family. One who came about 100 miles to see me was deaf and dumb young man (one of the family) who most of the family seemed to ignore. I could not speak the language anyway so me and him got on OK. He helped me to fix the bike a lot which was made in China and always going wrong. He was very good at fixing and mending bikes, you often get that with disabled people deaf and dumb, blind or whatever, they have inner strengths. When I came back to England I gave him the bike, he is now important, somebody, probably for the first time in his life.

I still send some money over to the family when I get the chance. Well that's my last three years. If you are interested in going further back in my life story you will have to write me another letter, even if it just says goodbye Keith I will not be writing again. I like to know where I stand.

PS Sorry about the bad writing

PPS You should write a book Sharon. Your letters are worth thousands. A book would be millions.

PPS As I have said, you can ask me ANYTHING and you will get a truthful answer in the end. What about you? Have you got any no go areas? I'll try you with one question. In Africa everyone had black skin but no one had black lungs, what colour are you?

I hope for a reply.
Keith

I still felt a little frightened especially because Mum had said he personally posted his letter. She was angry, he seemed to want to be my friend, am I portraying that I want to be his friend? Are his stories made up? Was he still trying to manipulate me? He is trying to have a joke with me about smoking and my lungs being black. I then moved to empathise with where he was, he is frightened of who I am showing the letters to, he still doesn't understand why I feel the need to share the letters.

I decided to write again.

Thank you for your honest reply. I feel I need to start with who I have showed your letters to as I feel this is maybe where you are most wary? My family and friends have seen your letters, however they have no input into what I write to you or if I continue to write.

As I have explained before, I am very fortunate to have a family and friends that accept me even though they may not understand my feelings and thoughts. I also feel that I need to be clear in what I am prepared to share. I get the feeling from your letter that in return for me knowing your story, you will want to know about my life? I have to be honest and tell you that I will not be disclosing any information about my family and friends. I am prepared to disclose my thoughts and feelings connected to you or on any disclosures you make if you want? I am not wanting to create a friendship connection. What I am offering and wanting in return is a connection that is very similar to a friendship (trust, acceptance, honesty) except for that it is mainly one-sided. I suppose I am asking you to give more? I question my last sentence because I feel that I am also offering a lot, I am offering a connection with acceptance, honesty and love where you will hopefully feel safe enough to share and be listened to within this connection. I suppose I am hoping we both benefit from this connection. You in that you will have an opportunity to feel accepted, supported and listened to, and me in the fact that I will hopefully gain truthful knowledge and understanding into possible developments of behaviour from experiences of life. I have not written to anyone else and I cannot answer your question of who might see these letters in the future because I do not know. If I felt that our letters were relevant to help others in the future then I could and most probably would use them.

Can I ask how much of the story about Africa resembles your life? Were you ignored by your family? Do you think you had a good connection with the young man because you could empathise with him in ways other than language? What really drew you to the old lady (I mean there must have been dozen of people selling fruit), did she resemble anyone?

Can I also ask that you do not post your letters personally.

Again I will understand if you do not want to proceed and thank you again just in case.

147

Keith responded:

Thank you for your letter. I start my reply at the end (of your letter) as usual and work backwards. Before I do, remember two things that have been said in our correspondence. There is a reason for everything and an excuse for nothing (ME), Equal control (YOU).

If I am to stick to mine, you have to stick to yours EQUAL control does not mean 70-30 or 60-40 but 50-50 or 100-100. Royal Mail is not owned by us (the public) anymore. Most of it is owned by million-aires. I don't like giving my money to rich people. Another reason I delivered the letters myself is that I do deliveries around that area so it is easier (and cheaper) to take them myself. Nevertheless, I accept your request and will post them in the future. Don't forget we are equal. Why do you not want me to deliver personally? Real reason please.

When we were walking to the market in Africa, there were a lot of people selling fruit as you say, but they all had friends and family with them. The old lady was alone in a black hole, mentally not physically. NO one cared if she died that day or the next day. She looked as if she did not care herself. I get an electric feeling from people (positive and negative) and I wanted to get her out of the black hole even if it was only for a short time. The deaf and dumb young man (Dan) was in a black hole himself but was trying to get out alone. I imagine you know the feeling, as well as giving him the bike, I would take him to the market with us (he just wanted some-one to show an interest in him).

24-01-14
Sorry about the delay. I have been overrun with work, family and personal problems. I do not watch television so I am not interested in false imaginary people, in soaps and game shows but just in real people who I know or I have met in my life. I have a good connec-tion with my sister in law who is in Africa at the moment. I am not interested in your family and friends so I will not ask any questions

about them. I am very interested in what you have been doing in the 15 or so years, but I have decided not to ask you any more questions so just tell me what you want. I get the feeling you would rather ask me questions than answer mine. I was well brought up as a child but without a lot of affection.

As I have said before, ask me any questions you want and I will give you a truthful answer or will say I don't want to answer that. I will do my best to not upset you or the 5-10 or 50 other people who read my letters.

Yours thoughtfully
Keith

PS if you want to help other people to sort out their problems as you have said. You will have to try and move in larger circles or you will not meet them.

I felt that Keith was frustrated and upset because there was restrictions on what I was prepared to share and in what way I wanted him to respond. I replied with what I was seeing.

Thank you for your letter. I get the feeling of frustration from your letter. I do not intend to cause frustration, I want to be honest and open with you. I am well aware of my passion for equal control, in my last letter I stated boundaries where I feel comfortable to go. I am not saying that I will not meet you as an individual but I will not meet you sharing other people's connections with me.

I feel that I need to explain this more for further assistance in your understanding of this. I am also aware of how my letters start with me and explain me but your letters do not. I don't mind this and I am fully aware that at the moment I am giving more, but again I feel comfortable with this so here goes.

I feel I need to respect others' confidentiality whilst writing to you as they might not feel and think the same way as me, so this is why I am asking if you will post the letters. I understand your frustration of unbalanced power within this world as I feel it too. I do not feel I have more control than you, you are free to also to set boundaries if you choose to and I believe I will respect and adhere to those boundaries.

I am also sensing a lot of frustration around people reading our letters. Does this make you feel as though you have no control? And if so why do you choose to write back? I can only give my point of view and I feel you are brave in writing and I appreciate this however I will again accept and respect if you choose not to respond.

You say that the lady in Africa was alone in a black hole mentally not physically, how did you sense this? What did it feel like? Could you see hope? You say that Dan was trying to get out alone, so does this mean that the old lady had given up? Do you perceive that Dan would have managed to get out alone?

The answer to your perception of me is correct. I do know the feeling of trying to reach the top of a black hole, trying so hard to understand experiences that hurt and are so painful and wanting help only to be met with more pain... so lost that you feel that there is no hope. Were you their hope? Did you want to be needed?

Keith didn't respond again, I was OK with this. On further reflection I became self-aware to understand that even though I said I wanted to contact Keith because I wanted a deeper understanding into his life and possible development of his behaviour, I actually also contacted him for myself, to show a part of myself, my brain, that I didn't need to be afraid of him no more, that it was him who was lost and frightened.

Chapter 16

New Love of Life

I had moved to apply in the first year of university to different placements and I wanted to connect with the NHS as I knew the training would be great and that it would look good on my CV. I used my skills that I had learnt while being a representative to prospect and wrote letters in order to be seen. I managed to get an interview with NHS working with adults and also an interview with Place2be working with children. I wanted a variety of experience to analyse and explore what the difference was, and I knew I would love working with both adults and children. I was worried was I taking too much on, would I be any good? I had started to listen more to my intuition which always told me that I would be fine and that I would reflect and change things if I wasn't OK. I got both placements which I loved and the training on both placements was amazing; the work with children seemed a lot more relaxed in structure, more freeing to use different mediums, play, creative work and the results where amazing to witness. Whilst working in the NHS it felt more rigid and controlled; there were set tools that needed to be used before I felt able to relax to just start counselling. I was on edge and nervous about getting things right.

About five months before I would start these placements I had started with another counselling company that offered free counselling to adults but I had to find my own supervisor. I had searched and researched myself for this supervisor and decided that I felt safe with her. I was sat in my car before our first session. I acknowledged that I felt nervous and a little anxious. I acknowledged that within my thinking I was putting my supervisor on a pedestal, building

151

to what I perceived to be outer power, where I was too focused on my supervisor's professional experience and academic knowledge which I feel internally was creating more power for my supervisor and making me feel weaker. I started to acknowledge that my supervisor was human and with this I also acknowledged mistakes she has made and would make, the time it takes to learn and the personal work that is required to grow. I started to build myself up with acknowledging my own personal growth, my personal and professional experiences and the learning that has come from these experiences. I felt that this process helped me to create internally a balance of power, equality. So when my supervisor pointed out that there was a power difference and how did I feel about that, I felt surprised but comfortable as I personally felt at that time for me there was no power difference. From my perception we were equal, so I was surprised that she felt there was a power difference. I expressed that I was fine and that I respect that she has more academic knowledge and counselling experience, however that I hoped to learn and grow from our interactions. I felt my supervisor was surprised by this, there were other things that I felt my supervisor was surprised about on many different occasions and from experiencing her reaction I had started to feel irritated. I looked deeper into my feelings and the process.

I considered that my supervisor was stuck in the definition of me being a student and I felt irritated that my supervisor wasn't seeing me in any other way. I expressed this to my supervisor and we had conversations on what the difference was, I felt better for expressing what I was feeling and why. A month or so later I explained to my supervisor that I had planned to join the NHS a couple of months' time so I would be seeing a total of five clients and that I would still need her for supervision for the clients I was seeing at the free counselling service, but that I had free supervision from the NHS. My supervisor's reaction was that she was surprised and then questioned me on what my plans were. I felt uneasy that she was searching, scanning me. I was honest and told her, she became defensive and explained that she was concerned that I was taking too much on. I explained to her that I felt safe enough to see more clients. My supervisor said that it was all fine with me feeling safe but she needs to ensure that my clients are safe. I expressed that I feel there is no difference, as I considered that if I am safe then my clients would be safe.

On reflection I considered that the difference was that I emphasise the importance of the 'self' in relation to everything, whereas I considered that my supervisor had a different view and for her, safety was in following what other people said and did. I considered that the construction of the role of a supervisor got in the way of our connection through the power that the role created, and if the person who held the status believed in that outer power. I considered that the responsibility my supervisor felt moved her to create what I considered rigid boundaries in order for her to feel personally safe. I felt that I wasn't going to be seen by my supervisor because of her fear, so I moved to discuss our issues with the course leader at University. I explained to Ben what I could see and why I thought it was happening. I explained that I was not just a student, that I had 36 years of personal and professional life experiences that I had reflected on and analysed myself. Ben understood where I was coming from and offered suggestions for us to be able to move forward. I presented these to my supervisor, who I felt created more outer power and referred to stages of what students go through regarding boundaries, and again went on to define me as being in the teenage stage.

I felt frustrated and acknowledged my own emotions and thoughts then I moved to empathise and search to try and understand what was happening with her. I considered that my supervisor didn't feel safe when her boundaries were questioned. I explained that it wasn't my intent to rebel, but that I was passionate about being seen for who I am and acknowledging myself in relation to my professional growth, that I felt I was on a lead and restricted. I explained that what frustrated me was in a year's time I would be free to see five clients a day five times a week and that I felt the boundaries she was putting in place were in fact dangerous as they were too restrictive; I felt it was safer for me to explore my ability while I was surrounded by people who could see me, my counsellor, tutors at the university and herself. My supervisor didn't want to or was too afraid to budge, so I came to the decision that I would finish at the free voluntary placement in order to work for the NHS. I had chosen to conform to my supervisor's boundaries but I was aware I was doing it. I figured that I could have gone and moved to get another supervisor, but my intuition was telling me that in between our interactions and experiences of each other was a lot of learning, about power, control and boundaries, so I stayed to learn more.

Within our personal development our group used to laugh at me always referring to outer power, control or rigid boundaries whether that was connected within personal interactions or as a society as a whole. I used to laugh at myself, but I couldn't stop seeing it or detecting it within things, and I soon came to realise that I was also fearful, sometimes controlling and had developed rigid boundaries especially regarding my children, money and household cleaning. I acknowledged that even within my thinking I had developed to blame, define and conclude experiences, things and people. I started to acknowledge when I would project out onto Adam or our children: you are making me angry, I would shout. I would observe them do it too and would voice what I was seeing, I would try not to project out and to manage my emotions better but it was hard and I would get so frustrated with myself. Why can't I just stop doing it?

With theory I would also get frustrated they would teach us one theory then another that contradicted the other theory; I remember thinking, well, who is right? Who am I supposed to believe? Ben would ask us to think for ourselves, asking us what did we think. What really frustrated me though was they wanted us to think for ourselves, but when it came to writing an assignment, they wanted us to tell them what all the professionals thought. I used to think to myself, what is the point in thinking for ourselves, when really, when it came down to being seen, no one is interested really in what we have to say as one individual, they only want to know what someone well known has said, someone with outer power, status or money – plus most of them are dead so really who gives a shit? We are the ones who are living. Who are we really following and why are we following them? Are we as a society just not stuck in the past? I redirected these questions to myself. Who am I really following? And why am I following them? The answers I received internally were really insightful. I was following people, family, friends, a culture, a society that didn't understand me and I was following them because I was frightened, frightened of not being loved, frightened of being judged, frightened of being alone, frightened of making mistakes. I acknowledged that I was alone, I did make mistakes, I was judged and I judged others too, and that most of the time I didn't feel loved. Why? I knew I was loved but why didn't I feel it? Soon enough I would find out.

Chapter 17

Full Circles, Endings and Healing

At this time Mum had separated from Barry, but before they split I felt that I had developed a better relationship with Barry, he had opened up more about his childhood and relationships with his children, and at times told me things he regretted. I could see his vulnerability, his confusion, his pain, I had more understanding. I opened up too about my feelings but I owned them, I felt this way, I felt that way. I think the breaking point was when my brother had given Barry a lift one night after he had been to the pub. Barry's friend jumped into the front and said, "OK John." Our John took that to mean they were both in the car so started to drive off, only Barry was only just getting into the back of the car and was dragged along the floor. Our John heard Barry screaming and stopped, but Barry had already scraped all his legs and was shook up. When Barry was telling the story to us all we couldn't help but laugh; he was getting angry and I felt that he was upset. I stopped laughing and started to empathise with him, saying that he seems upset. He said he thought he was going to die, I said it does sound a scary experience but that he has to see that it was also funny. Barry started to blame our John and said that he had finished with him. I started to feel upset and commented that I didn't think he should do that. Barry asked why I was upset. I said with tears in my eyes, "Because I know how it feels to be ignored by you and that it is upsetting." Barry seemed shocked and said that he thought John meant to do it. I said that our John wasn't like that, and he knew he wasn't. From then on, Barry seemed to want to talk to me, he had stopped pulling faces when I would visit Mum and he would stay and contribute within my and Mum's conversations.

I had also developed a more loving and open relationship with my Dad. A few years ago, Dad had returned a Christmas present that I had brought for him and Jane. I was heartbroken and all feelings came back from being a child and feeling confused, lost and not loved by my Dad. Dad returning my present was the last straw I needed to confront all my feelings and I decided I was going to write Dad a letter. Dad rang me to explain why they were sending the present back; I told Dad that I was really upset and that it had brought lots of memories and emotions back from being a child and that I was writing him a letter. Dad asked me not to write a letter and asked me to come and speak with him and Jane. I was scared. Could I do that? What I was feeling was so painful. Would they listen to me? Would I hurt them? Would this be the end of our relationship? My intuition was saying that I had nothing to lose, that I didn't have a relationship with my Dad at present, that this would be an opportunity to clear the air and build one. I loved my Dad and really wished that I did have a loving relationship with him. I missed him, I felt that I missed out on having a Dad growing up, the loss was so painful. I said that I would go and see him and Jane, my sister Sandy said that she would come along with me for support.

When we entered Dad and Jane's house I could tell Dad and Jane were nervous, they were busy cleaning around. I felt for them as I knew I too was really nervous. I asked them if they were going to sit down. They did, and Dad went on to explain that they sent the present back because they wouldn't have used it and didn't want it to go to waste. I said that by sending it back, I felt rejected and this feeling sat with a lot of memories from when I was a child. I explained different memories and my emotions connected to them, their interactions with me and that I felt I could do nothing right. I explained where I was at that time, that I was a child that was being sexually abused, emotionally and mentally abused, that I had lost my family and that I had nowhere safe to be. I would come to their house to be told we only went when we wanted something or to be ridiculed in lots of other ways. They were listening to me; Jane started to cry and she explained her story of where she was at that time, what she was trying to manage from her past and present. I could see her, that she was a 33-year-old that was trying to manage her own family issues, her own personal issues and met my Dad, who had four children and a wife who had asked my Dad to leave. I could imagine from her experiences and what she had said her insecurities, her fears, would my Dad go back to his wife whom he has four children to? Would my Mum want him back? Is this why she wasn't kind to us? Just like Barry, fear had gotten in the way; is this why we experienced all that we had?

Jane asked if I thought she was as bad as Barry. I was honest and said gently that she was. Jane cried some more. I felt for her. Dad kept quiet, my intuition was telling me this is what we do to each other when we don't acknowledge our emotions, when we don't know ourselves, when we are in pain, we project outwards just like Barry and Keith or we internalise and attack ourselves, like I did, like my Mum and Dad seemed to do, and we can move to do both. It felt sad, but also a big release, and empowering to now have understanding. We discussed more and I told them that I was thankful that they had listened to me, that I wanted to build a better relationship with my Dad, Jane said that we could visit whenever we wanted and that maybe we should come when she is not there so we get one to one with Dad. I started to visit Dad when Jane was at work, but I also visited when she was there, and on reflection I was building a better relationship with both of them. I wanted to build a relationship with both of them, I loved them both. There seemed to be an equal understanding between us all and all my childhood emotions I had managed to let go of.

It was coming close to me finishing university and I had gathered lots of hours counselling at NHS and Place2be. The experience was amazing; I loved the work and it was magical to see my clients move to understand themselves and change or heal. When I was working with the voluntary counselling I bumped into Rick; I had not seen him for years, the only other time was when I was with Adam and kids getting our car wheels changed. He said he was there testing the premises' fire alarms, and asked what I was doing. I looked a mess and was embarrassed to see him. We made small talk for a while and then we parted. I remember thinking, I hope he is happy, and wondered whether he was. I searched for him on Facebook and requested him as a friend, he accepted and I could see that he was married but now single. I remember thinking that it was a shame as I really expected him to be settled and in love.

The time came to finish university. I was sad to say goodbye to everyone, I knew that my attachments there with all the tutors and peers was what had helped me find and understand myself. Their acceptance and love had helped me not to be fearful of looking deeper to understand myself, and this then gave me personal power to move in a loving way to go back to people that I thought and felt had hurt me to gain further understanding. I was thankful and wanted to show them how thankful I was, so I wrote a poem. I had already told our course leader Ben that I felt more complete within myself, and I wanted him to know that I believed that the balance of his course and my attachments with the tutors is what helped me to become more complete. Ben became emotional and said that he appreciated that I had told him. My internal chat was, wow there would be no way I would have done this a few years ago, I would have thought it but would have been too frightened to express myself. I was so proud of myself and determined to express my gratitude to the other tutors; don't get me wrong, my thoughts were 'what if they think it's shit? What if they don't see me? People will think I am weak'. My intuition was saying that it didn't matter what others thought, it was important for me to show my gratitude to the ones who had guided me, and supported me, becoming more me. I wrote:

I know there are no words to express how much our connections mean to me so I will try to capture my meaning in my poem.

I feel freer, more alive, and more whole than I was before.

I now have more understanding and forgiveness of my past experiences and my decision to keep part of me secure.

I was stuck, shut away, lost in all that I had and was experiencing in life.

Filed away, kept safe in a hope that I wouldn't hurt no more.

I had tried to get out many times before, only to discover I had locked the door.

I couldn't remember what I had done or where I had put the key.

So there I was stuck and it was getting really hard to breathe.

Part of me must have known where I needed to be, because on my first day of the course I had already started to see.

I acknowledged and shared my feelings of feeling safe and secure and I expressed that being here was like coming home to me.

However I have to confess I was really shocked and surprised at first when I noticed you all had a key.

A key that I thought could potentially hurt me, but my heart on the other hand was shouting set me free.

I felt safer that none of you entered, you would all just visit and leave, leaving gifts outside the door for me.

However, I also felt frustrated, "how, why could you all not see" that I didn't have a key?

One day I started to wonder how I had become so stuck, that once you all had gone I started to open boxes slowly one by one.

I was amazed with what I had stored and what I could remember.

Some of the boxes started to disappear but others stayed the same.

Upon reflection I started to understand, that connected to these boxes was blame.

It was then that I realised I hadn't lost my key; the only person who could open the door, was me.

As trust developed between us I felt safe enough to move, then safe enough to pick up your gifts that helped me to choose.

As time passed by my confidence grew and I was able to bring out a box, then two, as I started to share I laid myself bare.

The feeling that I had felt that day, I had definitely experienced before, but how is it that I remember, as I was only about four?

I felt free in every way and so excited to explore, fearless of things people might say as none of you had ever banged on my door.

You all just listened and accepted me, my feelings and my thoughts. This allowed me to be free and to feel safe enough to explore.

I would come back with other boxes that I struggled to understand and together we would wonder about the contents in my hands.

I have learnt through you all, acceptance and forgiveness for myself and for others, through my understanding of why and how I became stuck. You all have helped me to move, helped me to love myself, and helped me to heal myself and through all of this I experience freedom, freedom to live and freedom to explore once again. Thank you, Ben, Kath, Ray, Peter, Dave, Paul, Julie. For helping me find my key, I am forever grateful.

I was excited to start to build my business and Adam was still working away. Adam had commented that he loved having time on his own while working away, which I could understand, remembering working in Butlins and Jersey. I had moved to create a professional portfolio, explaining who I was and what my history was. My plan was to attach to a couple of schools and develop a private client base as well. The schools would give me regular income while I built my name with attracting private clients, I had also studied Life Coaching and a Hypnotherapy course. I loved it all and started to apply it all within my own life. Paris and Jessica were growing and Paris was soon to start high school.

It was June 2015 and Adam had come back from working away; we still had a bit to do on house and Adam had decided that he was going to work with his brother. This would give him a regular income which was good money and he would have less stress. We had been busy doing our own things so we didn't have much time with each other of late. Adam commented that he found it difficult to connect back with me after he'd been working away. I sat down thinking, this is great, he is opening up to me, explaining where he is. I said that I felt we were distant from each other, we talked some more and as Adam said more I started to feel that churning in my stomach. I searched internally, my intuition was saying there was something more, someone else involved. I asked Adam if there was anyone else involved, he got angry and said no, that he thought I wanted it to be about someone else so it wasn't about me. I felt hurt. I told him my intuition was telling me there was more to what he was saying. Adam again denied that someone else was involved. I begged him to please tell me the truth, telling him that we had been together for over 14 years and that I deserved the truth and respect. Adam moved away and still saying that it was all in my head, that I was insecure and jealous. I started to question myself: was I? My intuition was telling me that I wasn't, that I needed to search. I looked at phone bills and reflected on previous conversations, there was a couple of things on his phone bill but nothing really standing out. I phoned different numbers, there was one which was a

24-year-old girl who was a stripper; she was the daughter of Darren, whom Adam worked with in Guernsey. Adam had mentioned that Darren's daughter was going over while Adam was over there, which I thought nothing of at the time. I did have a dream that Adam was having an affair with Darren's wife, but I thought again that maybe I was feeling a little insecure that he was away.

Adam had phoned this girl a few times but nothing that would give me concrete evidence. I phoned Ella and told her the story; Ella said she thought I was insecure. My intuition was shouting at me 'you are not'; I moved to talk with Mum. Mum said he had done something. Mum came to our house, she wanted to see Adam for herself. Adam seemed to avoid her. Mum said, "He has cheated, Shaz." I was crying within. Even though I knew what my intuition was telling me, I still didn't want to believe it as I knew it would be the end of everything. Mum helped me to confirm what I already knew. All that we were supposed to be creating together, all that we had been through, all that I had given, our children and our extended families, I just saw pain and lots of it. The problem was I knew what I knew but I still had no evidence. I had gone to Adam with what I had gathered and he had answers for why he rang Darren's daughter. I couldn't rest, felt upset and cried when Adam was asleep. I didn't want him to touch me. I reflected on our time together, and all the lies but also all the great times. My intuition was saying that Adam was and is a great guy, that we have never been on the same level/page, that we are at different development stages physically and spiritually, and that I deserved to find someone who can truly love me like I can love them, someone who can offer me what I can offer, someone who will compliment me as I would them. After a few weeks I decided that we were over. Adam had said he had felt this way about us since January and we were in June and he was just telling me. I explained to him I wanted to be with someone who could and wants to communicate what they were thinking and feeling; Adam seemed shocked and also relieved, we both cried. Adam had said that he thought it was for the best as well as he wanted his independence. We discussed that Adam would move into the garage once it was completed, and then he would look to eventually buy a house close by so the kids would have us both close.

I moved to tell my family and Adam told his. It wasn't long after this that Adam had come home from work and I was outside having a fag; that gut feeling wouldn't go away. I said to myself, I know what you are telling me, but what use is knowing when I have no physical evidence to prove to everyone else that I am right? Everyone is just going to think I am insecure, and with that something just told me to look in his van. Adam's door was open and there was another phone in the side drawer. I was shocked; my heart started pounding as I scanned through it. Lots of phone calls to a girl called Sandy, and Darren's daughter, plus messages since April 2015. I was angry, but my intuition knew that I needed time to gather the evidence first and understand myself before I reacted. I was outside and phoned Sandy. I explained calmly who I was and told her that she needed to get herself checked sexually because Adam had been sleeping with other people. Sandy said it was a work thing, nothing happened. I said calmly, don't lie, there are messages on there saying I will meet you in the hotel. I explained that if she was married or had a partner that I suggest that she tell them as I will find out who she is, and with that I put the phone down. I phoned Darren's daughter and left a message as she didn't answer. I heard a bang on our window. Adam was stood there, looking really angry.

I went in and said to Adam, "Come on, we need to look at the garage," as our children were watching a film. Adam followed me down the garden and said that I was a sneaky cow, I laughed trying to hold my anger and said the only one sneaky here is you, who the fuck are you? I don't know who you are, I have been with you for 14 years and I really don't know who you are. Adam said it was just sex, I laughed again and said oh, it's OK then. I explained to him that to me it is not just sex, it's no trust, no honesty, no communication and no respect. Internally I felt and acknowledged my anger and was able to tell him that I was more angry that he had been trying to get me to go against myself, my intuition, moving to put blame on me. We spoke some more. I knew I still wasn't getting the full truth but really I wasn't that bothered at that time. Adam asked what happens now then. I said the same, you move into the garage. I wanted Adam around for our children, knowing it was already a lot for them to digest that their parents we were not together any more and that things would be changing. I wanted a smooth transition for them, and for us to be honest with them about what was happening. I phoned everyone and told them what my intuition had been telling me was true, everyone was shocked.

I remember being on the stairs upset, crying, and my intuition asking, what am I doing? Other thoughts were that it was sad everything was ending, Adam had cheated again. I asked myself, do I really want to be with a guy that cannot communicate and be honest? I didn't; I would rather be on my own. With that I got up and went to bed. Adam continued to live with us, I found it really healing as I was able to go back to him to find answers to my questions and Adam seemed honest about where he had been and where he was. I could see within his answers that we were so different, and when I asked him why he didn't communicate, he said well, you were controlling. I asked him to explain further, in what way, as I didn't want to go into another relationship not understanding. Adam said he was afraid, I said in what way, he said he was afraid that I would leave him. I said to Adam, don't you understand that I have always been honest with you about what I wanted from a relationship, and that could he not see that he has chosen to conform himself to be the man that I wanted because he wanted to be with me? That I believed in him doing this made him feel controlled, but I believed I haven't controlled him, that he had done that to himself. Adam didn't get it, or didn't want to, but I did, so it didn't matter whether he did. I wasn't going to crucify myself with all that he was projecting. I would still check myself, meaning if what he was saying had truth and some did, but I didn't crucify myself, I sought within to understand further. Adam would still try to have sex with me. I told him he had no chance, that he would never see my body naked again, I would shut the door when going to the toilet or in the shower which he thought was funny, but it was over and there was no way I was giving him an opportunity to try to get back.

I remember sitting for a month, reflecting and looking where I was, where I had been and where was I now going; what did I want from my life? I was still having counselling which was great and my family and friends were great support. I wrote down my ideas, my feelings, things that I was stuck on that had happened within our relationship and I would go back to Adam for answers. I would move to talk with family, everyone was worried and thought it was weird that I was still allowing him to live with us, but my intuition was telling me it was important. I had made a decision that I was going to listen to my intuition from now on rather than others. Finding that phone was empowering, empowering that I had stayed with myself, that I had not been influenced by Adam in what he was saying, and others in that they thought I was just insecure. People would say you both are OK now, but wait it will all kicks off and it's bound to turn nasty at a later date. My intuition was saying it doesn't have to be that way, there are two children in the middle of us and I promised myself that I would always seek to understand myself fully and then move to understand Adam in order to avoid conflict. That didn't mean I needed to give in, just find words to explain myself emotionally and cognitively and my actions, or what I was witnessing. I knew from all my life experiences that I had no control over anyone else only myself, and my control came from understanding where I was emotionally, cognitively and then intuitively. To express myself through my intuitive analysis of everything.

Adam would come back and ask what had I been doing all day, I told him I was healing. After a month I started to move and sent my portfolio out. Adam had said he would still pay for bills while I got work. I managed to get work within a school counselling children; the head of the school seemed to understand why I used play therapy and she said she believed in therapeutic interventions which was great. I felt nervous. This was my first paid job being a counsellor, I loved working with children. I had two that I was told were really challenging and that they would disrupt classes and run off constantly. I would watch teachers be in a panic. I felt worried. Was I going to be OK, would I be able to help these children? My intuition was telling me to only take this work on for now and to learn everything I could from being in a school environment, the teachers and the children. To analyse it all, the structures, interactions, emotions and cognitive behaviour and how the school moves to try to regulate children's behaviour, that this experience would somehow be important in my future, plus I had a lot to look at personally, so to take my time.

Chapter 17

Self Development
and Facing Fears

I knew I had fear of dating again, but my biggest fear was sleeping with another man. My thoughts were that my body has changed, I have had two children and put on weight. I knew there was no way I wanted another relationship, that I wanted time to ensure that my children were safe, time for me, time to figure out who I am just being me and not attached within a relationship. Adam had come to me to say he was scared about dating again, we had a chat about it and I said sometimes you just need to push yourself to see that there is nothing to be scared of. I helped him set up a portfolio on Match.com. Again, everyone thought we were weird, but at this point I knew I didn't want Adam as a partner, that I loved him and wanted him to be happy, that all that he had done he hadn't meant to do, he just didn't understand himself. I knew this from my own past movements of creating drama that when we are not self-aware we move and create situations that create drama and pain, because we don't understand ourselves. It wasn't long before Adam started dating; he would come back and tell me what they were like, we would laugh and think it was really funny that we could do that with each other. We had conversations about when either one of us gets another partner that we would promise each other that we would always put our children first, that there would always be communication between each other. Adam had slowed down on getting the garage completed as he was going out enjoying himself. I started to feel irritated. I explained to Adam that I wasn't prepared to keep this arrangement for long, him living in the house, dumping his clothes and me still taking responsibility for everything. Adam moved more on the garage and about two months after separating

Adam met his new partner, who was a friend of Adam's friends. Adam told me about her, that he really likes her. My stomach was churning again. I asked Adam if he had ever met her before. Adam said he had seen her a couple of times when out with his friend. My intuition was telling me that more had gone off between Adam and this girl while we were together. I remembered a dream that I had about Adam's friends being at our house and some conflict was going off, I was upset sat on the stairs and it was Christmas time. I wondered if this was trying to tell me something? My thinking was even if something has happened between them while we were together, does it really matter now for me to search to find out? I decided it didn't matter; what had or hadn't happened was irrelevant to where I was now, I didn't want him as a partner, so I let it go.

Adam continued to date his new partner and always seemed to be out, not getting on with the garage. I started to get more frustrated and angry. I acknowledged that he was taking the piss, using our house like an hotel. I checked myself to ensure I wasn't jealous. I wasn't, I acknowledged that I was frustrated that I couldn't move on while he was still living in our house; I was still the responsible one. In October I told Adam he had to be in the garage for the end of December or that he would have to go and live at his Mum's. Adam said that I was just jealous. I told him he could think whatever he wanted but that didn't change the fact that I wanted him to move out. I explained where I was and pointed out to him to see how reasonable I had been about the whole situation. Adam did start to move more with the garage but it soon faded off again.

Paris and Jessica kept coming back to us to understand why we didn't want to be together any more. My intuition was to be completely honest with them about all of our relationship, but Adam didn't want me to tell them that he had cheated. I explained to Adam that we don't have to create blame and that the truth always comes out in the end, and that I was worried that then it would cause our children not to trust us. Adam was adamant that they didn't need to know that. I discussed it with my Mum, who agreed with Adam. My intuition was telling me that they should know everything without blame. I was in internal conflict. My thought was, well, it's not that I wanted to keep a secret, so Adam will have to deal with this at a later date. I told my truth to Paris and Jessica, that I believed Adam and I loved each other and that knew I always would but that we weren't in love with each other. I explained it in other ways, such as it was a little bit like them with their friends when they fall out, that they still care for their friends but don't want to play with them any more. I explained that there were differences between Mummy and Daddy which would cause us to fall out, sometimes I was wrong and sometimes Daddy was wrong but that didn't mean we didn't love each other or them, and that our love for them will never fade or go away. I reassured them that when their Dad does move out, they would have equal time with us both and that I know they love us both equally the same.

There had been a few changes in our Paris's behaviour, like getting really upset about a friend moving; she had asked if this friend could live with us as she didn't get on with her family. When I explained that could not happen, Paris became uncontrollable, screaming and crying, saying she was going to run away with her. I was worried. Paris had started high school, so there was a lot of change happening there as well as at home. I expressed my concerns to Adam, who said I was looking too much into it but my intuition was telling me different, Paris was struggling. I explained to Paris what I was going to do and why. Then I moved to tell the school our situation and her behaviour. Everything that I could see and that I wanted support for her, so she had someone outside of the family to speak to about anything she was struggling to understand. I explained that I was a counsellor but I knew she needed someone who was not emotionally connected to her, to feel safe enough to look. The school was great and put in group work and one to one if she felt that she needed it; Paris's behaviour got a little bit worse to start off with, but soon settled.

I had gone out a few times with friends and one night while out I got chatting to this guy. He was lovely, we had a really good conversation, and I found him physically attractive. He invited me back to his house. I was in internal conflict. I knew that I needed to sleep with someone to get rid of my fear, but was I ready? After a while, I decided that I was and that it was just going to be an experience, great conversation and sex. I was really honest with this guy about where I was and what I wanted, and he seemed fine with that. We had sex and that was just what it was; afterwards I said that I needed to go, this guy was shocked and asked why I wasn't staying. I explained that my children were at home and I needed to get back to them. We chatted for a while afterwards and he was honest telling me that he felt used, I said that I was sorry but that I was honest about where I was (coming out of a 14 year relationship) and what I wanted (as in a sexual connection). I explained that I thought he understood this; he said he did, and to call him at a later date when I am ready to date. I said I would and then I left. I felt like I had done something wrong. Thoughts were, what are you doing, you are a mother, not 18 again. I was struggling to accept that I had just had sex with another guy as if I had cheated on Adam. I acknowledged it was because he was still living with us that I still felt responsible for him.

The experience of having sex with that guy helped me to know that I would be comfortable with my body to have sex with other guys, but I also knew that I didn't want to just have sex with anyone or sex alone, that I wanted a deeper connection, but also I didn't want a relationship. I moved to tell my friends. Some were shocked and said they couldn't understand why I would want to have a one night stand. I explained where I was, most of them had more understanding. I was worried about what they would think of me but my intuition was that they were all in different places to me and as long as I was OK with it, it didn't matter to what other people would think. Ella would say that I shouldn't tell people everything, but I told her that I am not shutting down and hiding myself again. That these people were my friends and family, that I wanted a deep open and honest relationship with them, and that if I wanted to be honest then I would. If people want to judge then they can, but that I knew from my own past experience when I judged it said a lot more about me than it did about the person I was judging.

It was November and Adam was nowhere near completing the garage. Adam came at the end of November to say he was going to be moving in with his new partner at her Mum and Dad's house just before Christmas. I was shocked and asked him if he had really thought about it and wondered whether he thought it was too fast. I also asked him if he had thought about our children, with it being Christmas, and how this would impact on them. Adam said that it wasn't fair on his new partner that he was still living with his ex-partner, and that she had been OK about it but now both of them had fallen in love with each other. Adam said that he would come back on Christmas Day to be here when our children open their presents, but that he wanted to introduce them to her before then and for our children to spend time with them both over Christmas. I said that I thought it was quick, but it was up to him. Even though I was shocked, I wasn't shocked that he was moving in with his new partner as my intuition told me that he would move that way. I was shocked at the speed and the lack of consideration for our children. I was aware that I felt anxious about our children meeting Adam's new partner, but I was unsure where these feelings really sat and whether there more feelings that were underneath it all. I knew I needed time to reflect and work out where I was emotionally and cognitively about what was going to happen. We agreed that Adam would continue to support the house and bills till February to give me more time to get more work, then he would pay maintenance and half of the mortgage till our children were 18. My intuition was saying this wouldn't happen, that Adam wouldn't continue to commit to paying for the house till our children were 18, but I went along with what he was saying.

Afterwards I acknowledged that I felt nervous and anxious about our children meeting Lisa because of my experiences with Barry and Jane; I didn't want my children to experience what I had. I also knew I had no control over what Adam chose to do, that he was their father as well as me being their mother and I wanted our children to have a great relationship with both of us. I had learned lots from my own life experiences and I admitted to myself that I also felt a bit jealous of my children building a relationship with Lisa and Adam without me, that they would have another life. I remembered being a child when my Mum and Dad separated, all I wanted to do was to love everyone and for everyone to love and get on together. I told myself that my children will love me no matter what, and I wanted to create that balance and for them to love whoever they want to love. I didn't want to dictate to them who they should love. I wanted my children to be happy, I wanted Adam to be happy, and I wanted to be happy.

Our children met Lisa and they came back excited, explaining to me what she was like; our children liked her. I could see through what they were saying that she seemed really nice, and I relaxed more. Adam moved out. I promised myself I would always try to be aware of any of my emotions that would come up, and that I would always move to explore them and my thoughts and listen to my intuition so that I had more self-awareness. I had realised that this process gave me understanding, acceptance and self-control into how I reacted to situations and people, I also acknowledged that I was starting to feel happier and freer as I was starting to feel more complete...

Awaken

Oh my God! Where have I been!!
Have I been living in a dream?
I feel I am awakening from my daze,
Opening my eyes and now willing to embrace,
A wholeness within, but I am unsure where to begin.
What I know is that I must share my story as I unfold,
Which I feel connects me with a story untold.
A story that connects me with thee, and thee with We.
To which I feel is yet still to be disclosed.
Understanding I feel is the key,
then comes acceptance of me and then of thee,
with empathy 'I' becomes a 'We'.

Who was I? A 8-year-old girl that had love, peace and happiness
that I wanted to share with others. I had privileges, not in that I
had money or status, but in that I had attachments that showed me
unconditional love – my mother and my family. I believe we all
lost our way through painful experiences, becoming disappointed,
angry, jealous and disillusioned. Who am I now? A woman who has
privileges, again not in money or status, but in finding attachments
(who were strangers to start with: friends, teachers, ex-partner,
tutors and my counsellor). Through them giving me their time to
listen to me, my story and accepting all of me, my thoughts, emotion
and behaviour so that I could understand myself within my painful experiences past and present, developing my intuition, these
people's past and present interactions with me helped me to heal

myself... I will never forget my guardians and I am eternally grateful but I will always remember that I am... my saviour.

Next book... Working Towards Complete Freedom

CPSIA information can be obtained
at www.ICGtesting.com
Printed in the USA
LVOW11s2141130318
569713LV00001B/94/P